HARDY, WOODY PLANTS FROM SEED

HARDY, WOODY PLANTS FROM SEED

P.D.A. McMillan Browse

GROWER BOOKS LONDON

Grower Books
50 Doughty Street
London WC1N 2LP

First published 1979
Reprinted 1980, 1985

© Grower Books 1979

ISBN 0 901361 21 6

Designed and produced in Great Britain by Sharp Print Management, Manchester

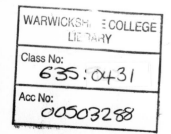

Contents

Appendices

Part II
Encyclopaedic list of Genera

Foreword

These notes have been produced as a response to requests which have been received over the last five or six years, from many practising plant propagators and students of nursery practices for information on the production of ornamental, hardy woody plants from seed. These requests have usually been coupled with an appeal for a recommended and relevant source of information. Apart from the U.S.D.A.'s 'Woody Plant Seeds Manual' of 1948 and its long awaited successor 'Seeds of Woody Plants in the United States' eventually produced in 1975, there is virtually no one work with practical relevance which can be confidently commended, and even so these works only deal with plants grown in the United States and under their, albeit very variable conditions.

It therefore seemed that the provision of some sort of reference should be undertaken in the belief that there is need for a source of information covering both production under British conditions and the extraordinary variety of subjects which are produced from seed in the Nursery Stock industry in this country. However, the author acknowledges his own limitations and lack of competence to undertake such a work in this field, but in the absence of any alternative exponent of this technique of plant propagation the task has been undertaken with a real enthusiasm. The necessary academic exercise of researching, surveying literature and seeking advice has proved most rewarding, as has the continuing practical aspect of the task.

The prime motivation (apart from the author's own egotistical reasons) for attempting to produce such a book has centred on the provision of information for students reading in the field of nursery practices, as these individuals are so woefully short of any practically applied textbooks in almost all aspects of their production technique. This does not intend to suggest however that the needs of the commercial plant propagator have been any the less relevant in choosing material, for these two groups represent the same people in successive generations — todays students being the working propagators of tomorrow. It is also my hope that horticulturists in general will find the material useful whether they be lecturers striving to keep abreast of techniques in a dynamic industry; advisory officers needing an alternative source of information or professional gardeners who may be called upon from time to time, to propagate such plants from seed. Finally I am also aware that it may be of value to the competent and knowledgeable amateur gardener who wishes to produce hardy, woody plants from seed.

Because of the present limited state of available practical knowledge and information, these notes do not pretend to be definitive or authoritative, or to offer a complete answer to the propagator who wishes to grow a wide range of woody plants from seed. They represent an attempt to assemble relevant and reliable information for British conditions which the nurseryman can use with some confidence, as most of the material emanates from the writer's own experience and observation. Similarly the encyclopaedic list of plants which constitutes the second part of the work does not pretend to be a complete coverage of all subjects grown from seed in the United Kingdom and no doubt it will be the absentee subjects which will frustrate most readers as they have the writer! The subjects included have been limited to those plants whose propagation can be described from the writer's own experience and observation: as it would have been an unwise, within the context of a publication such as this, merely to cull through unverified data and present information from already existing sources. This procedure would simply perpetuate some fallacies and erroneous statements and in the long run prove confusing and ultimately frustrating. Most observations presented have therefore been verified from experience or are otherwise qualified by comment within the text. It is also hoped that these notes will prompt other propagators to communicate with the author so that faulty statements and conclusions may be corrected, or further information added so that a fuller, more useful and valuable body of knowledge may be assembled.

Some of the information used in this volume has previously appeared in the 'Gardeners Chronicle' and the 'Nurseryman and Garden Centre' and I am grateful for the permission of the respective editors to use this material here.

It is not expected that all readers will agree with the thoughts, ideas and systems postulated but it is hoped that these will be accepted as a basis for discussion, amendment and development.

With this latter thought in mind I offer my sincere thanks to my colleagues Peter Hutchinson, Richard Chandler and Stuart St. John who from time to time have endured my continuous questions and discussions with good humour and have contributed much to the overall development of the ideas expressed in these notes. Finally, my thanks to all those students who at one time or another have helped me to formulate the basic systems and to those practising plant propagators who have never failed to provide advice and information when asked for help.

Brooksby Agricultural College,   *P.D.A. McMillan Browse*
Melton Mowbray,
Leics.
Summer, 1978

PART I

1 Introduction

The main theme which has prompted the appearance of these notes on such a specific subject at this particular time, is dominated by the fact that certain cultural and economic pointers and indications within the industry suggest that the current uncertainties of the international trade in nursery stock will continue to increase — at least for the time being — and as this uncertainty prevails there will be an increasing demand for home produced material. As much of the cheaper sector of this trade is in woody plant seedlings for growing on, rootstocks, etc. it would seem prudent to expect an expansion in this field of production.

Such new production would necessarily be expected to develop on a sound economic base, and this is only feasible if accurate and useful technical information is available to ensure that the fundamental system of production is sound, and in consequence allow a planned and co-ordinated enterprise to be established.

The present situation has developed because it has been the traditional practice of the British nursery stock industry to import seedlings from european sources, but the present economic climate and financial uncertainty has turned these normally cheap and readily available plants into expensive and unreliable items. It is this uncertainty on which the British producer must capitalise in the short term to produce a home based trade.

At the time of writing the chief problem is caused by the continual fluctuations of international currencies, and this is further aggravated by the present trend to 'float' a currency. This effectively means that forward pricing as far as the buyer is concerned cannot be firm, indeed the values of a currency may vary dramatically between the placing of an order and its delivery and invoicing six to nine months later. These difficulties are also aggravated by the costing problems associated with inflation which can arise in such a long term transaction. Because of these financial uncertainties the supplier will understandably be disadvantaged and he will look for an alternative and financially more reliable market. This consequently introduces an element of unreliability into the supply situation.

A decline in grading standards and general quality reflects the increasing labour costs of the producer on the continent as he also struggles with inflation. The demand for availability for early season planting and the limitations of the continental climate have also dictated changes in his *modus* 1 *operandi* which has led to such techniques as defoliation, cold storage and all the attendant difficulties which this produces.

These limitations and uncertainties are compounded by an increasing home based demand caused by the current vogue for quasi-natural and environmental plantings, coupled with the requirement for a wider than traditional range of subjects. The importation of certain genera has long been restricted on phytosanitary grounds and it is quite feasible that with the increasing trade from eastern european sources that the range of subjects prohibited may well be extended, as a protection against certain non-endemic pests and diseases.

In toto it would appear that the home production of a wide range of woody plants from seed could become an expanding enterprise as a result of these pressures. A market is therefore developing for the production, locally, of ornamental, hardy, woody plants from seed. With the added advantages that the crop is not affected, other than marginally, by the vagaries of the weather; for which delivery can be expected with some certainty at a fixed and reasonable price; and of a quality which can be readily inspected before sale.

1.1 GENERAL CONSIDERATIONS

The propagation of a wide range of woody plants from seed presents an extremely varied enterprise, as the diversity of virtually all the aspects of production, which are involved, militate against any generalisations or standardisations of operational technique. Indeed it is difficult to visualise any general factual statements made in relation to seedling propagation, which do not require qualification of some kind, when applied to a particular subject.

In the production of hardy nursery stock in the United Kingdom, the propagation of woody plants from seed is generally still operated as a highly traditional enterprise relying on established technique and experience. In contrast much has been achieved in recent decades in furthering and enhancing our knowledge of the majority of aspects of vegetative plant propagation and indeed our Victorian forefathers would probably marvel at the simplicity, sophistication and fundamental understanding of our various techniques and systems of environmental control, when dealing with that aspect of plant propagation. Our usual methods of outdoor seedling production would, however, show few basic differences from the systems of production with which they were familiar.

The propagation of woody plants from seed has received scant effective investigation from a practical operator's viewpoint for a few hundred years or more, so that it is not surprising to find that few practical advances have been made in the methods employed in this field of propagation. It would, however, be unfair to suggest that work has not been in progress or that significant advances in knowledge have been limited, for much fundamental and even applied research has been undertaken on the physiological and biochemical aspects of seed biology especially. But for the practical propagator who is concerned with immediate field operation and the actual production of the crop, little work of day to day value has been forthcoming or at least communicated in an available and comprehensible form. In practice the propagator is still using lengthy and traditional procedures for overcoming seed dormancy, sowing at random rates and husbanding the crop virtually only by visual observation.

It is only in very specialised crops — such as the production of rose rootstocks — that any real application of research findings have been transposed into effective field scale operations, however in fairness it has probably been the pressures of economic necessity which have produced a situation in which such limited application of available information has been effected; for too long the production of seedlings, in the nursery stock industry, has been regarded as a cheap and almost second class system and economic production has not been a fundamental essential.

Many nurseries grow woody subjects from seed but still, in general, give the operation little thought except perhaps in terms of mechanisation and labour usage. All too often one observes seedbeds with either too high a population of valueless seedlings, or far too thin a stand to produce an economic return. Basically this situation is due to lack of knowledge and often to an absence of an understanding of all the factors involved in seedling production. Even seeding rates are usually merely culled from unrelated forestry publications or out of date and unreliable horticultural sources, and in practice are determined without any reference to the capability of the seed sample itself or the required end product.

In attempting to assess the correct procedures for seedling production from the available literature, the propagator usually encounters a mass of, often unrelated and confusing, facts. It is, therefore, important to visualise the process of propagation of plants from seed as a logical sequence of events which requires just as much thought, planning and preparation as any other technique of plant propagation; so that any particular piece of knowledge or information can be placed in its correct context.

Information on various specialised aspects of seedling propagation is available from a wide range of sources, both horticultural and scientific. However, the problem for the propagator is to find and assemble these facts, be able to discard those which are of little value or are confusing, and correlate those which are useful. So that as a result he may determine a system of production for any particular woody plant. In practice this situation presents a problem which is almost insurmountable for the average propagator to overcome, as the diversity of these sources of information makes even their assembly a difficult task, even without superimposing the personal inclination of the propagator, his available time or his abilities in assessing their value.

Because the propagation of woody plants from seed in the nursery trade should of necessity be a commercial operation, then one of the primary considerations in deriving or assessing a particular system of production must be the economic aspects of the entire process.

In general terms the ideal system of seedling propagation entails the production of the greatest number of acceptable seedlings from as small an area of seedbed as can be reasonably achieved, and that the seedlings should occupy the seedbed for as short a period as may be feasible.

The determination of acceptable costs of production for ornamental 3 subjects must obviously be within a budgeted income and this will inevitably be compared with data from forest tree nurseries as these are virtually the only figures available, and a basis for comparison will be sought. Although these figures may have some relevance in the large scale production of hedging plants and rootstocks, it must only act as a platform when considering the various systems of production for ornamental subjects. Woody plants of ornamental subjects are generally produced individually on a smaller scale than forest tree subjects, but as they represent a considerably higher value it is more than possible that they will warrant a greater investment in terms of materials and time to ensure the production of an acceptable end product. Thus their costings will bear little relation to the low input/low output enterprises carried out on a large scale, as is experienced in forest tree nursery practice.

One of the major problems in dealing with relatively small quantities of a wide variety of subjects from seed is the great diversity of so many aspects affecting production. Factors such as seed morphology with its almost infinite variation in physical measurement and characteristics, as well as the range of season of seed maturation and the types and combinations of seed dormancy, all militate against any uniformity of operation and all these factors present their problems when attempting to standardise systems of production. Because of these difficulties it is not easy, for example, to develop a system of mechanised precision sowing which would be compatible with the accurate distribution of such types as *Abies, Acer, Castanea, Araucaria, Clematis, Halesia* and *Rhododendron,* and in consequence sowing is usually by hand. However, mechanisation has proved feasible in the preparation of seedbeds and in crop spraying, as well as undercutting at harvesting time.

In the production of a crop of seedlings it is also necessary from the practical aspect to know from where seed can be obtained, how it should be stored, how it should be dealt with to ensure satisfactory germination, how satisfactory seedling populations are achieved and subsequently how the seedling population should be managed.

The object of the exercise however is to produce a crop of seedlings of adequately similar characteristics, within the median range of variation which represents the characteristics of a particular species or variety. Thus attention to the selection of the parent plants is of some considerable importance in relation to the genetic capabilities of the proposed seed sample.

In all but unusual circumstances the production of seeds in woody plants is as a result of the process of sexual reproduction. This in itself implies the occurrence of genetic variation, however limited, within a population of seedling offspring, for this system of reproduction ensures in this way the survival of species should conditions change. From a horticultural standpoint those variants which are of interest are very limited and the crop needs to be as uniform as possible.

The greater proportion of ornamental woody subjects which are to be considered in these pages show only limited variability, with the vast majority of the population being 'typical' in their characters. Even the inherent variation within a species, variety or ecotype is usually negligible in practical terms provided that natural and usual pollination has occurred.

Some variation is almost bound to show up, but in practice the production of a desired seedling crop can be achieved by roguing in the seedbed in order to produce an acceptable sample.

The main causes of a high level of unacceptable variants in a population of seedlings can usually be attributed to faults in pollination, either as a result of self pollination when cross pollination is normal, or pollination by other adjacent plants of suitably related species with the production of a hybrid, and therefore variable population. It is for this latter reason that the value of trees in the arboretal situation should be carefully assessed before being used as sources of seed.

Although the term 'seed' will be used throughout these notes, it is used purely for convenience to describe the propagule, in all or part of its dispersal unit, of a flowering plant. The true seed may well be enclosed within several layers of 'fruit' which often remain right through until germination.

In nature the chances of the seed germinating and developing into a mature plant are infinitessimally small. Pregermination losses are enormous through the action of feeding birds and animals, pests and diseases, unsatisfactory environmental conditions, etc. Once past that stage the germinated seedling has to survive vast changes in environmental conditions, pests and diseases, browsing animals and competition from other plants. The object of an artificial system, such as is practiced in a nursery seedbed is an attempt to identify these losses, isolate and control them where this is possible so that a potential maximum number of seedlings are produced from the available seeds. Seed germination and seedling survival in nature is obviously therefore a highly improbable activity, which it is the plant propagator's problem to understand, modify and improve upon.

GENERAL READING

Anon (1948) 'Woody Plant Seeds Manual', U.S.D.A. Misc. Publ. *654,* U.S. Govt. Printing Office.

Anon (1961), 'Seeds', U.S.D.A. Yearbook of Agriculture, U.S. Govt. Printing Office.

Anon (1975) 'Seeds of Woody Plants in the U.S.', U.S.D.A. Agric. Handbook *450,* U.S. Govt. Printing Office.

Barton, L.V. and W. Crocker (1948) 'Twenty Years of Seed Research', Faber and Faber.

Barton, L.V. (1967) 'Bibliography of Seeds', Columbia Univ. Press, N.Y.

Burbidge, F.W. (1877) 'The Propagation and Improvement of Cultivated Plants', William Blackwood and Sons.

Crocker, W. and L.V. Barton (1953) 'Physiology of Seeds', Chronica Botanica, N.Y.

Hartmann, H.T. and D.E. Kester (1975) 'Plant Propagation — Principles and Practice', Prentice Hall, N.Y., 3rd Edition.

Heydecker,W. (ed.) (1972) 'Seed Ecology' Butterworths, Oxford.

Kozlowski, T.T. (1971) 'Growth and Development of Trees', Academic Press, N.Y.

Kozlowski, T.T. (ed.) (1972) 'Seed Biology', Academic Press, N.Y.

Wells, J.S. (1968) 'Plant Propagation Practices', Macmillan, N.Y., 3rd Edition.

2 Sources of Seed

Seeds can be obtained either by collection from particular local sources and personal contacts, or from the usual range of commercial seedhouses which operate throughout the world.

The local collection of seed has much to recommend itself as a general practice. It is possible, under these circumstances, to ensure that the proposed parent plant(s) can be positively identified, and that some assessment can be made of the likelihood of cross pollination from other species, as this may induce a degree of hybridity and in consequence prejudice the value of the seedling population. It is also likely to provide seedlings which will prove hardy in that particular geographical area. Experience has shown that seeds from warmer areas may not be sufficiently hardy, while material from colder climates may not grow to reach the levels attained by seedlings from local sources, although they will exceed growth rates for their normal environment. Some assessment insofar as it may be of value, can also be made of the potential of the plant in terms of its desirable characteristics as a parent.

The location of mother plants within reasonable proximity also allows the propagator to determine the likely level of cropping in a particular year, well in advance of collection, so that deficiencies can be catered for from other sources. It, in addition, gives the propagator the opportunity to collect the seed at that moment of maturity which is deemed to be the most desirable.

It is not easy, however, for any one propagator to obtain all his requirements from that local catchment area which he is capable of servicing, either because of the time factor or because of the quantities required. Under these circumstances it is necessary to call upon the assistance of reliable personal contacts who will obtain seed in their locality under the same stringent conditions.

If this still does not complete the requirements, then recourse to the available commercial seedhouses should be made for supplies. These houses have the advantage that, as wholesale agents, they are able to offer an extensive range of material which they assemble from widely scattered areas. Because of the quantities involved, the necessity for some uniformity of storage conditions for the wide variety of types, and the ability to transport them easily; as well as the time scales involved in collection, organisation and

6

dispatch; it is probable that the viability of the seed sample will almost certainly be influenced to its detriment to some degree. Similarly, it is not always possible to rely on the supply of seed in any particular season, or on its accurate identification, until it is too late to compensate for it. Nevertheless, these firms are a useful adjunct to the nursery trade and a very necessary aid to the propagator who needs to produce a wide range of ornamental subjects from seed. A selection of such seed houses is listed in Appendix 1.

The implication that the local collection of seed provides a panacea for all previous difficulties would be ill founded, for as a bald statement it ignores many of the practical implications and problems. For *if* seed bearing plants are available, what are the factors which determine recognition of those plants which will produce the most desirable seedlings? Does age, size, position, etc. of the parent plant influence seed production in terms of quantity and/or quality, or does isolation, or close stand position of the parent plant affect the genetic complement of the subsequent seedling populations? All these factors, as well as many related considerations, must be recognised by a propagator who anticipates collecting his own seed and expects to obtain a useful seedling stand. However, as it is unlikely that the commercial seed collector will have paid any particular attention to this sort of detail either, it is probable that a sample from a commercial seed house will not perform any more successfully than the home collected material.

Some knowledge of the occurrence of good seed is also very relevant as quality of seed will necessarily affect seedling stands. Having satisfied all the other factors in the terms of seedling production, it is pointless to start the process with a sample of seed which is less than satisfactory in any of its characteristics and attention must be given to these fundamental considerations.

Much could be written about the provenance and the selection of the source of seed in relation to forest tree subjects, but in the context of ornamental subjects it has little significance as any choice of source is not widely available.

In forestry terms the geographical and climatic origins of seed is termed its *provenance* and this is strictly controlled by national agencies and to some extent by international agreement. In ornamental seed catalogues such information is usually lacking, although some seed houses do indicate countries and even areas of origin of a seed sample: this is especially true of North American suppliers and latterly to the Danish sources especially.

2.1 INFLUENCE OF THE AGE OF THE PARENT PLANT ON SEED PRODUCTION

It is not always possible to determine with any degree of precision at what age a plant of any particular species can be expected to produce useful seed crops. However, it can be assumed that, under normal circumstances, a plant will pass from the juvenile phase of development into the mature phase (and therefore be capable of seed production) at a definite age. This age varies extensively from species to species even within a particular genus, but variation within the species is usually within reasonably narrow limits. 7

During the initial period of the mature phase, the plant will continue to grow at a fairly vigorous pace and this vegetative extension growth is produced at the expense of seed production. Normally woody plants do not start to develop prolific crops of seed until they reach middle age, that is the period when the plant has reached the greater part of its ultimate height and spread. At this stage extension growth has moderated and there is an accompanying increase in the propensity to produce flowers. It is not possible to indicate with any accuracy at what age this particular stage will be reached, as it represents a function of the growing conditions experienced by any individual plant; for trees of similar age growing in differing conditions may well react differently. A tree growing in good soil conditions with a satisfactory climate will continue to grow vegetatively with a continual annual increase in size for many years, under which circumstances seed crops are usually poor, whereas a tree of similar age growing in poor soil or adverse environmental conditions may soon cease extension growth of any significant vigour and start to produce relatively large seed crops albeit from a small tree.

Some knowledge of these particular aspects of development will be of significance to the propagator who may wish to establish seed orchards, so that some idea of the time factors involved can be determined.

2.2 SELECTION OF THE PARENT PLANT

When comparing individual plants of a particular species of a woody subject as possible sources of seed in terms of their observable and desirable physical characteristics, the available evidence tends to suggest that in a natural population these factors have no measurable effect on the growth, development and characteristics of the ensuing seedling population. Any differences in vigour of the seedlings can be attributed rather to seed size and quality than to the direct genetic influence of an individual parent. Height, shape, size, etc. of the parent plant do not therefore necessarily have any affect on the variations which occur within the seedling population, although this aspect has not been clearly assessed for ornamental subjects. Nevertheless, in order to reduce any undersirable genetic variation it has been the usual practice of most propagators to select parent trees of desirable characteristics, for those characters which are visually apparent and easily observable, *viz.* good shape, requisite size, typical vigour, good ornamental characters and local hardiness. Many sources claim that mother plants can be selected to provide a more acceptable seedling sample but there is little available conclusive data, especially for ornamental subjects, which supports this argument. This does not preclude the possibility that some propagators have been fortunate enough to determine certain particular source trees of good characteristics which have produced seedlings in character, and the evidence of forest tree producers especially in the United States does suggest that the qualities of an individual seed producing tree are a good indication of the quality of the offspring and that good parent trees are likely to pass on the desired characteristics. This is especially true for certain species where particular characteristics are known to be inherited regularly, viz. straight stems in Oak *(Quercus robur)*.

In real terms a system of progeny testing each mother plant, however crudely it is recorded, is the only way of assessing the parental influence of the mother plants. Indeed this has been done most successfully for forest tree subjects.

The main problem in relating parental characteristics to their expression in the offspring is associated with the actual growing situation of the parent plants. If the parent plant is isolated or well separated from its neighbours it may well develop its full character and can be assessed for desirable characteristics as a parent, but in consequence may suffer from poor pollination by virtue of its isolation. An isolated specimen in an arboretal situation may also be subject to cross pollination from other species with consequent hybridity in the offspring. Plants in single species stands (where pollination is most effective) however, do not invariably have a chance to develop 'Typical' characteristics as age, density of stand, relative dominance of the individual, injury, etc. will all limit the development and the actual appearance of the plant. The seed from this type of source will therefore be collected from any reasonably acceptable specimen, but in practice it is usually found that only the dominant and co-dominant plants seed at all well as they are intercepting the greater part of the light.

One factor which may well have relevance within a population of mother plants is resistance to disease — it being wise to select seed from disease-free specimens in the *hope* that this character may be inherited.

2.3 FACTORS INFLUENCING QUANTITY OF CROP PRODUCTION

The quantity of crop produced by any particular plant in a season is necessarily a function of light, as available food reserves which can be allocated by the plant for seed production will reflect the photo-synthetic activity of that plant, and the chief limiting factor to this metabolic process in plants in the U.K. is light. Primarily however it is a function of tree size — that is the number of branchlets available to produce flowers and fruits. The amount of crop produced annually may also be influenced by other factors such as periodicity which will be discussed later. The climate in any particular season will influence crop production and the effects will be fairly obvious — a hot summer will induce high carbohydrate level for good seed production; poor pollination conditions reduce the possible crop, cold temperatures at critical periods may cause seed abortion, etc. However, it is the marginal effects which produce interesting situations — *Acer griseum* is often reported as producing more viable seeds at the top of the tree rather than on lower branches: this may be due to greater light interception with the consequent carbohydrate availability or perhaps because on nights when radiation frosts occur cold air drainage causes damage to the fruits on the lower part of the tree while the top is left above the danger zone. Similarly a specimen of the Hornbeam *(Carpinus betulus)* which was well sheltered by surrounding shrubs produced poor seed at the top of the tree where it was exposed to frost, while the lower branches developed large crops of good seed where they were sheltered. These reasons are speculative but the effects are evident and should be accounted for when assessing seed crops.

2.4 **FACTORS INFLUENCING THE QUALITY OF SEED PRODUCTION**

Seed quality is also an assessment of the vigour of a sample, insofar as it is a measure of the rate of seedling growth, and is affected by a number of factors. The most obvious of these is seed size, the bigger the seed, the bigger is the initial seedling and its subsequent growth rate. Size is normally a function of stored food and in consequence relative embryo size: all of which, if seed size is increased, enhances the chances of survival and the rate of seedling growth.

Quality may also be an expression of genetic complement. In nature most trees are geared for cross pollination, however isolated specimens may self-pollinate and normally this is reflected in a high proportion of malformed and aborted seeds together with low seedling vigour and a high proportion of undersirable seedling variations.

Trees still in a vegetative phase of development produce seed of less reliable quality as there is less available carbohydrate for seed development, most of it being used in vegetative extension growth. The same factor being responsible for poor quality in the 'off' years of those species showing periodic seed production.

Quality of seed is also affected by pest infestations such as *Megastigmus* flies in many conifers, weevils in acorns and other nut type seeds, chalcid wasps in *Sorbus,* etc.

2.5 **PERIODICITY OF SEED PRODUCTION**

The periodicity of good seed crops is a well observed and documented phenomenon especially in trees. The production of a prolific seed crop only occurring at, more or less, regular intervals. Some knowledge therefore of the years when a full seed crop is likely to be produced is important to the propagator in order that he may be able to collect sufficient seed, in excess of his normal annual requirements, in these productive years so that he is able to compensate for the deficiencies of the 'off' years by storage, and so ensure a continuous availability of seed annually.

Hartig at the beginning of this century suggested that good mast years in Beach *(Fagus sylvatica)* were a function of an increasing build up of stored carbohydrates in the stems to such a level that a full crop of seed could be developed. In subsequent years with the drastically reduced carbohydrates in the stems rebuilding slowly, the tree only permits the production of light crops until reserves have been restored to levels required for a further heavy crop. Although light crops of many subjects are produced in the intervening years, the seed is often of poor quality, it is low in stored carbohydrates, does not store well, is of low viability and produces seedlings of poor vigour. It is often also heavily infested with pests. Under these circumstances the seed is not worthy of collection. However, periodic seed production is not only a function of available food supply, it may also be affected and influenced by other factors.

Inherent genetic characters may affect the phenomenon — such as the biennial bearing of certain apple varieties, although not a great deal is known or understood of these influences.

Periodicity is usually fairly regular but it may be affected marginally by climatic conditions. Frost at a crucial stage in flowering or the early stages of fruit development may cause crop loss even if carbohydrate levels are satisfactory. Warm summers with high light intensity will induce good carbohydrate levels and in consequence flower bud initiation. Conditions at pollination time, however, may influence the degree to which successful and extensive fertilisation occurs. Thus because of the diversity of factors involved fluctuations from the normal are usually limited.

ASSOCIATED READING

Faulkner, R. (1967) 'Procedures Used for Progeny — Testing in Britain with Special Reference to Forest Nursery Practice', For. Comm. For Rec. *60*.

Heit, C.E. (1967) 'Propagation from Seed 4: Importance of Seed Source', Amer. Nurs. *125*(2) : 12.

Kennedy, J.N. (1974) 'Selection of Conifer Seed for British Forestry', For. Comm. Lflt *60*.

Scanlon, D.H. (1976) 'Seed Source Effects on Sugar Maple',Amer. Nurs. *143*(1) : 13.

Seal, D.T. Matthews, J.D. and R.T. Wheeler (1965) 'Collection of Cones from Standing Trees', For. Comm. For. zrec. 39.

Westwood, M.N. (1966) 'Arboretums — Note of Caution on their use in Agriculture', Hort. Science *1*:85.

Wyman, D. (1953) 'Seeds of Woody Plants', Arnoldia *13*.41.

3 Seed Storage

The maintenance of an acceptable level of viability within a seed sample at an economic cost until it is required for propagation, is one of the major factors in the successful production of woody plants from seed. For those seeds which can be harvested from good crops annually and which will experience little delay before sowing this consideration provides few problems. But for those plants which are periodic in the production of good crops of seed, it is necessary to store seed during the intervening years in order to provide regular annual availability of supplies. In order to do this successfully and provide seed of high viability each year, some provision in the form of storage is necessary and a knowledge of the factors governing this aspect of the environment of the seed will be required if quality is to be maintained at acceptable levels.

3.1 VIABILITY OF SEED AND ITS ASSESSMENT

The chief interest, in the collection, extraction, storage and processing of seeds under commercial conditions, is in the effects these activities will have on the level of viability of the finished sample at the time of sowing, and it is obvious that any unnecessary loss of viability during these phases makes the surviving proportion more expensive.

In assessing the value of a seed sample, quality is not only a measure of genetic complement and level of stored food reserve, but is also a function of the viability of each individual seed.

The viability of a seed sample is an expression of that proportion of the sample which is alive at that moment at which the determination is made, and hence is a measure of the potential number of new plants which could be produced if the seed was to be germinated at that time.

The term 'Longevity' is often encountered in the context of viability and this measure gives an indication of that period over which the seed will survive and during which a particular or acceptable level of viability will be sustained. Basically this factor is a function of an inherent characteristic but is also marginally influenced by storage conditions.

Although seed can be kept or stored satisfactorily with some knowledge of the expected or potential longevity of a particular seed sample, it does not provide any indication of the effects that a lengthy period of storage will have on the 'vigour' of the process of germination. For the longer the seed is stored the lower will be the remaining food reserves and in consequence the rate of germination and seedling establishment will be slowed and this may have profound effects in the seedbed where a depression in germination vigour may cause a marked decline in the number of those seedlings which survive and establish.

3.11 MEASURE OF VIABILITY (see also Appendix IV)

However, what is of importance to the propagator is how the proportion of viable seeds can be recognised, as it is only this part of the sample which is of value to him. Any technique which provides an assessment of any decline in quality will also be of value.

The viability of seeds can be determined in a number of ways — the simplest and most useful, from a practical standpoint, is an ordinary *germination test* which measures not only those seeds which will germinate, but by assessing the germinated proportion at certain time intervals, an assessment can be made which gives a picture of the 'germination vigour' of the sample. This simple system which obviously requires fairly controlled environmental conditions is only of any value when the seed has no dormancy factor or the dormancy factors blocking germination have previously been eliminated. Since, however, the period of germination for many woody subjects is often relatively lengthy it may not prove a satisfactory technique to use after dormancy breaking treatments as it may delay sowing for too long a period.

For those seeds which are of an adequate size and have a reasonably large embryo, viability can be assessed by the so-called 'Cutting Test'. For this determination a sample of seeds is opened and a visual assessment can be made of those which are alive. Some idea of quality can also be obtained, with experience, by determining the amount and distribution of necrotic areas in the seed. This condition is usually prevalent in samples of freshly collected seed from 'light' crops or increases progressively with the length of storage even in apparently sound seed.

The third available test is the 'Tetrazolium Test' which is based on treating the opened seed with a dye which is taken up by living plant tissue of the embryo. This is a relatively sophisticated laboratory test which gives an accurate measurement of viability because only living tissue is stained. Vigour can also be measured according to the quantity and situation of dead material within the seed. It also has the advantage of providing a measure of viability in dormant seeds and seeds with small embryos. Results are assessed visually as the dye makes measurement simpler by enhancing a contrast, making it simpler to observe with or without magnification.

3.2 PRINCIPLES AFFECTING SEED STORAGE

In order to maintain a useful degree of viability in a seed sample, some knowledge of the conditions necessary for their successful storage is required. This entails an assessment of the environmental conditions which will enhance the length of time at which acceptable levels of viability will be maintained.

In practice this is achieved by slowing certain metabolic processes within the seed which are essential to continued life, but which can be reduced without detriment. The length of a successful storage period will be a function of how much these processes can be affected. In effect storage is achieved by slowing down the process of respiration in the seed, preventing the deterioration of stored food reserves and by immobilising certain essential enzymes, etc. Storage may also be regarded as a period in which the embryo is maintained in a quiescent state and the environmental factors affecting germination are reduced to an accepable minimum.

However, any period of storage must have a deleterious effect on the viability and quality of a sample over a period of time. Under normal circumstances, without any artificial storage control, a sample of seed will show the typical fall off in viability which is expressed in the graph below and any storage controls merely attenuate the curve thus maintaining viability over a longer period.

3.21 WHEN TO STORE

Attention to the curves of the graph also indicates another major effect in successful storage. The object of storage is to attempt to *maintain* a level of viability for as long as possible with any loss reduced to minimum levels. It is therefore imperative that storage must commence at the earliest possible practicable occasion after collection. Under these conditions the highest feasible level of viability is initially present and can subsequently be sustained. By its effects storage delays the deterioration in viability levels of a sample, but from the graph it can be observed that this rate of loss is not constant and once the steep part of the curve is reached the rate of deterioration does increase dramatically, hence the importance of commencing storage early (high on the curve) in order to give as long a period as possible before the more rapid period of deterioration begins.

Thus in order to obtain the maximum effect from storage, seeds should be processed and stored as quickly as possible after collection so that intitial viability is high and the *rate* of deterioration is decreased.

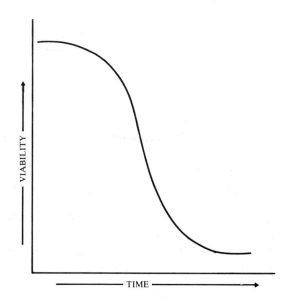

This graph represents the decline in viability of a sample of any seed during time. The actual figures and units for each parameter will vary for individual species and the 'Time' factor may vary from a few days to several years.

The value of the graph as a picture is to emphasise the importance of subjecting the seed to the storage environment as early (i.e. as high up on the curve) as is feasible in order to maintain good levels of viability for as long as is possible.

3.22 ENVIRONMENTAL CONSIDERATIONS

In practice storage is achieved by decreasing the rate at which certain metabolic processes occur and this is normally done by:—

(i) lowering temperatures so that the rate of biochemical reaction is curtailed. Normally one would expect chemical reactions to double in rate for every 10° C rise in temperature and conversely halve for every reduction of the same decrease. Most plant biochemical reactions are effectively slowed to very low levels at 5° C and any decrease in this level although marginal can be extremely effective. However, the affects of temperatures below 0° C are not well documented and although some seeds are known to survive freezing, in many cases it would appear to depend on the developed hardiness of the sample and on the speed of temperature drop;

(ii) considerations of the moisture content of the seed. A reduction in the moisture content of the seed is effective if it is to below a level critical for the mobilisation of certain water soluble materials and so reduces metabolic activity. However, the picture is further complicated by the levels to which desiccation can occur in particular seeds and this is influenced by other considerations such as the type of stored food — fats especially degenerating if moisture levels are even marginally reduced;

(iii) modification of the storage atmosphere surrounding the seed. It would appear relatively easy to reduce levels of respiration if oxygen is limited but it is only effective if the seed is dry, otherwise anaerobic reactions may occur. Practically it is not easy to provide a suitable facility for controlling the composition of the atmosphere.

As has been intimated, the longevity of a seed sample in storage is influenced by the temperature at which seeds are stored and their moisture content during this period. Harrington has devised a rule of thumb which postulates that in broad terms for each 5° C drop in temperature the life of the seed is doubled and that for each 1% decline in seed moisture content seed life is also doubled. He also indicates that both these factors interact down to a critical threshold by reducing the rate and effectiveness of 'Biochemical' reactions. This threshold is determined by the degree to which the seed is capable of withstanding reductions in these environmental factors, i.e. the ability of the seed to tolerate desiccation and its hardiness.

Storage of plant material is often effected by reductions in the level of atmospheric oxygen but in seed storage this factor is of minor significance when compared with temperature and moisture levels, although increases in carbon dioxide concentrations may have more influence.

For successful storage the seed must be 'mature', that is with a developed and quiescent embryo and a stable food reserve.   15

It may also be relevant to indicate that fungi will be active at moisture contents of more than 12 to 14% even at relatively low levels of temperature; and precautions, such as seed dressings, may be necessary to prevent losses by rotting under these circumstances.

3.3 METHODS OF STORAGE

The object of successful storage of seed samples is to enhance longevity, that is to maintain greater levels of viability than would normally exist without artificial aid. Although much has been written about seed storage there is little available information for the propagator of ornamental woody plants who wishes to store relatively small quantities of seed and does not have access to equipment for determining moisture content, etc. However, a few generalisations can be made which have proved successful for storing the following broad categories of seed types.

3.31 NUT TYPE SEEDS

Those genera and a few odd species which produce nut type seeds, often store a fair proportion of their food as some form of lipid, and in association with this have a high moisture content at dispersal. This type of seed degenerates rapidly on drying and even a marginal decrease in moisture content may cause a massive decrease in viability. Storage of these seeds must therefore be carried out on freshly harvested seed and storage conditions must arrest the process of deterioration as far as it is possible. As moisture content is critical this, in storage, will be a function of the humidity of the atmosphere and hence this must be sustained at a high enough level. Control is therefore achieved by a decrease in temperature.

These seeds are most effectively stored on the nursery by sealing them in a polythene bag (in order to maintain moisture levels) and placing them in a cold store at 1° C - 4° C. As it is possible for some fungi to cause problems, even at this temperature, it would be advantageous to dress the seed with a suitable fungicide.

Seeds benefiting from this type of storage will include; *Quercus, Castanea, Fagus, Aesculus, Juglans, Carya, Nyssa, Corylus, Lithocarpus* and *Acer.* Many other seeds which have traditionally been stored dry have been shown to benefit from similar conditions, as although they will withstand a greater degree of moisture loss than those listed, serious losses of viability are encountered if the moisture content drops below a critical level. Seeds in this category include *Fraxinus, Liriodendron, Carpinus* and *Pterocarya.* The majority of conifer seeds will withstand fairly severe desiccation but exceptions which require similar storage conditions include *Gingko, Abies, Cedrus* and *Picea.*

All the seeds so far listed would be considered only for a relatively short term of storage, in the case of *Aesculus, Juglans* and *Castanea* probably for only one year — a subsequent year showing a considerable deterioration in quality. More stable (apparently) types such as *Quercus, Fagus, Acer* and *Corylus* will store successfully for three or more years. In the case of this particular seed type decrease in temperature towards 0° C will increase temperatures.

3.32 SEEDS WITH HARD SEEDCOATS

This type of seed is probably the most easily stored as provided it is kept dry it can even be stored at normal ambient temperatures for considerable periods. This type of seed is already at a low moisture content at dispersal and although it can be dried further for an enhanced storage period, this may also increase the durability of the seedcoat.

The majority of subjects commonly encountered in this category are members of the *Leguminosae* such as *Robinia, Gleditsia, Gymnocladus,* etc. while others such as *Koelreuteria, Cornus mas* and *Hamamelis* exhibit the same characteristics.

Normally seeds of this type are collected at or about dispersal and stored in sealed dry jars at normal temperatures, although beneficial effects can be obtained by maintaining lower temperatures during storage.

3.33 OTHER SEEDS

The remainder of seed types are stored after drying, and storage requires the maintenance of low moisture content usually at normal temperatures. Low moisture content is normally between 4 and 6 per cent. Under these conditions storage is short-term but if stored at low temperatures longevity is dramatically enhanced. Most other woody plant seeds can be effectively stored in this way and this is especially true of the majority of coniferous subjects, which respond well to desiccation and, in which condition, store well even at relatively high temperatures (10° C): although *Abies* and *Picea* have been shown to withstand sub-zero temperatures for long-term storage.

ASSOCIATED READING

Barton, L.V. (1953) 'Seed storage and viability', Contrib. Boyce Thompson Inst. *17* (2): 87.

Harrington, J.F. and Douglas J.C. (1971) 'Seed Storage', Nat. Seed Corp., New Dehli, India.

Heit, C.E. (1967a) 'Propagation from Seed 10: Storage Methods for Conifer Seeds', Amer. Nurs. *126* (8): 14.

Heit, C.E. (1967b) 'Propagation from Seed 11: Storage of Deciduous Trees and Shrubs', Amer. Nurs. *126*(10): 12.

Roberts, E.H. (1972) 'Viability of Seeds', Chapman Hall.

4 Germination of Seeds

Having considered the factors which influence the production of a useful sample of seed and how it may be stored to retain maximum productivity, the next necessity is to have some knowledge of the requirements needed for inducing these seeds to develop into a crop of seedlings. These requirements are best described as the influences which reawaken the embryo from its quiescent condition to continue its development until its establishment as a new plant. Understanding this process will determine correct seed treatment, seedbed preparation and sowing to be carried out to their best advantage in terms of productivity and so enhance crop production.

The basic process by which a seed becomes a new plant is termed 'germination'. Definition of this process is somewhat difficult as it is a nebulous concept covering a wide variety of interacting physiological processes and environmental factors over a relatively lengthy period. For practical purposes, however, it can be defined as the process by which the embryo expands and enlarges, eventually emerging from the seed, and until its establishment as an integrated self supporting individual.

At the dispersal of the seed, germination is normally prevented by the ripening process, which occurs during that period prior to dispersal. During the maturation of the seed, moisture is lost to a level below that required by the seed for germination to occur. The water content of the seed is decreased to such an extent that the agencies governing the germination process are immobilised.

In this relatively dry, quiescent state the seed is comparatively easy to handle, extract or treat without incurring extensive damage, and in this condition is capable of some period of storage for as long as germination can be prevented and vitality maintained.

If no other blocks to germination exist and the embryo is merely quiescent the process of germination will be initiated whenever sufficient water is available to be taken up and the remaining environmental factors are suitable. Most woody plant seeds usually have some form of control mechanism which prevents germination until certain conditions have been satisfied. These mechanisms have evolved naturally to ensure the survival of the plant from generation to generation so that seed will not normally germinate either during or until the passing of conditions which may prove unsuitable for the survival of the seedlings. Seeds possessing such a mechanism, which inhibits the process of germination, are described as being dormant.

Thus before a seed will germinate two sets of factors must be satisfied:

(i) that all the necessary environmental conditions are favourable and:
(ii) that the seed is capable of immediate germination.

4.1 ENVIRONMENTAL FACTORS

The environmental factors influencing germination are well known and documented, thus it is sufficient to note that the process of germination chiefly depends on the availability of sufficient water, adequate diffusion of atmospheric gases (chiefly oxygen) and that the rate of the process will be a function of temperature.

Water is required initially by the seed so that the necessary soluble food materials, enzymes, etc. can be mobilised and the growth processes can commence. Most seeds take in water over a wide range of stress, but obviously this ability will be limited should the tension approach the permanent wilting point and at this level germination will be retarded. In the first instance water uptake by the seed is by colloidal adsorption and as materials become mobilised and active growth commences, it is taken up by osmosis. Ultimately water has a significant role to play in virtually all the growth and developmental processes and hence avoidance of any extensive degree of water stress is paramount if seedling growth is not to be checked.

Germination as a process represents a rapid increase in cell division and differentiation and as such depends on unimpeded respiration for the provision of the required energy. For the maximum release of energy and the most efficient utilisation of food reserves, respiration must of necessity be aerobic and the requirement of oxygen diffusion at the most efficient rate is of utmost importance. It is possible however, for seeds to respire without oxygen for short periods, but energy production is poor and the use of food material is inefficient, but this ability does permit a germinating seed to survive temporary periods of waterlogging as may happen in an open ground seedbed during periods of the winter.

The control of temperature in open ground seedbeds is not possible to any significant degree except that by choice of site, provision of shelter, etc. These effects may cause temperatures to increase in the spring and at an earlier date than would otherwise occur. Temperature not only affects the rate of seed germination but also the season at which the process will commence, higher temperatures which can be induced by aspect, site, shelter, etc. not only produces rapid germination but also advances the time of emergence to an earlier date, so potentially extending the growing season.

Although exposure to light or indeed absence of light may be a requirement of germination for some subjects, it does not appear to be a significant factor in the germination of the greater number of seeds of woody subjects except in the case of some freshy collected coniferous subjects e.g. *Tsuga,* and native Birches at varying temperature levels. Light sensitive seeds are only responsive to the stimulus when fully imbibed.

19

4.2 DORMANCY OF SEEDS

When a seed is subject to the favourable enviromental conditions it requires for germination, it will normally germinate, but if despite this situation it will not respond unless certain particular pre-determined conditions have been satisfied, then it is said to be dormant.

Although presenting an irksome problem to the nurseryman, this phenomenon is a natural defence mechanism which the plant has developed to ensure survival in the seedling stage. It will normally ensure that germination does not occur during, or immediately prior to the onset of adverse climatic conditions.

In broad terms the dormancy of seeds of woody plants of temperate regions can be attributed to a number of different factors but these can be categorised from a practical viewpoint into the following three groups:—

(i) those effects which cause a physical limitation on the process of germination by:

(a) preventing uptake of water
(b) restricting gaseous exchange
(c) limiting embryo expansion:

(ii) immature embryo conditions:

(iii) those conditions which are basically chemical in their mode of action and prevent germination by inhibition of an essential reaction necessary to promote germination.

Much has been written about the types of dormancy and their classification, from the basic system derived by Crocker (1916) to the generally accepted standards of Amen (1968) and the above is necessarily very similar to these.

4.21 SEEDCOAT DORMANCY

Seedcoat dormancy may be caused by the development of a hard seedcoat which effectively causes physical limitations on germination or by an impermeable seedcoat effect which simply prevents uptake of water by the seed.

4.211 HARD SEEDCOATS

A hard seedcoat causes the prevention of germination then by physical limitation. This may be manifest by a reduction in the rate of diffusion of oxygen, the limitation of water uptake or the restriction of embryo expansion. If such seeds are sown and left in the seedbed under natural conditions the seedcoat will gradually be broken down by the normal decomposing agencies of the soil. As might be expected this action is only effective during moist and warm conditions. Eventually the seedcoat will become reduced to a level at which these restrictions are no longer limiting and as the thickness of the seedcoat declines below the critical level those various physical activities which are necessary for the promotion of germination are able to commence. From the practical aspect, germination of such a sample of seeds (if the seeds are merely sown without pretreatment) will be erratic, both over a number of seasons and throughout each season; as within any sample of hard seeds there

seasons and throughout each season; as within any sample of hard seeds there will be marginal variations in 'hardness' and the rate of decomposition will be dependent on its immediate local environment. As this would be a very undesirable situation in commercial practice it therefore requires the pretreatment of the seed to ensure an even and uniform germination. This is aimed at reducing the seedcoat to below that level at which it is effective in preventing germination and can be achieved by any of the following techniques:—

> (i) *Scarification* of the seed is achieved either by agitating the seed with an abrasive grit or by passing the seed through sand or emery paper rollers until the seedcoat is physically rubbed away.

> (ii) *Chipping* of the seed is effective if the seedcoat can be broken or chipped easily and if the individual seeds are large enough to handle for this purpose, and in consequence is limited to subjects such as *Gymnocladus*.

> (iii) Reduction of the seedcoat by digestion with concentrated acid or other suitable reagents is extremely effective especially on very hard seeded subjects which do not respond to physical attack. However the technique requires a great deal of expertise if the seedcoat is to be effectively reduced and the embryo and foodstore left un-damaged. (see Appendix 3. 1 'Seed Treatments'.)

> (iv) If the seedcoat is not very hard, reduction of its effect may be achieved by soaking in warm water for a reasonably long period. The best results have been achieved by pouring boiling water (about two volumes) over the seed and leaving it to cool in a warm place for some twenty-four hours. This has proved effective for freshly collected samples of *Gleditsia*, *Cercis* and *Wisteria*.

4.212 IMPERMEABLE SEEDCOATS

This type of effect is often difficult to distinguish from the foregoing and is frequently combined with it. The impermeability is caused by a water repellent material which permeates the seedcoat and/or pericarp: it is usually an organic agent of the fat or wax type. Under natural conditions this type of dormancy is relatively transient as the normal agencies of decomposition in the soil are fairly easily able to reduce these substances.

Treatment of the seed to ensure a rapid and even germination is merely a question of extracting the causative agent, this can be achieved either by a hot water soaking as described above or by extraction with a suitable solvent such as alcohol or acetone, although dilute inorganic acids are normally effective also.

4.22 IMMATURE EMBRYO CONDITIONS

Dormancy which can be attributed to an immature embryo condition is fairly straightforward in that germination will not occur until the embryo has reached the stage at which it is fully developed and ready to germinate. Immaturity of embryo may be due to the existence of a rudimentary embryo which requires anatomical and morphological differentiation to reach the mature phase at which germination will occur and usually this particular condition is associated with the parasitic habit, although not exclusively so — *Ilex opaca* being an example of a normal woody subject in which the embryo remains rudimentary.

Immaturity, however, may simply be a question of size — the embryo although fully differentiated requiring a period of enlargement to bring it to the mature phase. This is well exemplified by *Fraxinus excelsior*. To overcome the condition the embryo requires a period of exposure to warm temperature, but as cell division and differentiation will be involved, *the seed must be fully imbibed and adequately aerated* so that the increase in temperature is effective in allowing the continued and effective cell division and differentiation. This effect can be achieved either by mid or late summer sowing or by summer stratification.

4.23   COLD TEMPERATURE DORMANCY

The seeds of many plants from cold temperate climates exhibit a dormancy condition which can only be overcome by exposing the seed, in an imbibed state, to a period of cold temperature. The mechanics of this type of dormancy are somewhat obscure although they appear to be concerned with either the processes involved in the mobilisation of stored food and/or chemicals inhibiting or promoting embryo development; the alteration of the chemical balance being achieved by a certain specific degree of cold. The level and duration of cold temperature required to produce the effect varies from species to species in broad terms, but in any particular seed sample there is also a marginal variation and from year to year for samples from the same parent.

Seeds exhibiting dormancy of this type appear to owe the mechanism of germination control to the presence of an inhibitor which prevents the process of germination from occurring. During the process of chilling however the levels of growth promoter in the seed increase so that eventually the effects of the inhibitor are nullified and germination can proceed, concurrently the levels of inhibitor in the seed do not as a general rule change although in some subject the level does decrease. Dormancy then is governed by a balance between the inhibitors and promoters, when inhibitors are dominant then dormancy occurs. It does not appear that there is as yet any satisfactory explanation for the role of chilling in altering the balance of these materials or initiating the appearance of the promoters either from their precursors or *de novo*. In many subjects the growth promoter present in the seed is of the gibberellin type and this factor may have a future use in breaking dormancy. Other workers have found very similar results from experiments in which cytokinin acts as a growth promoter in the same way.

It would appear simple to treat a dormant seed with gibberellic acid to overcome dormancy but the picture is complicated by the fact that over fifty naturally occurring variants of GA are known and growth promotion in each species may well be controlled by a combination of two or more of these, thus the logistics of this individual determination are extensive.

In the majority of woody plants showing this type of dormancy, the cold requirement is relatively small and as long as the seeds are in an imbibed condition, exposure to an average winter's cold will cause the inhibition to be overcome.

In this context 'cold' represents temperatures below 5° C and if necessary a sample of seed could be placed in a cold store in an imbibed state (say mixed with damp peat) to accelerate the process. However, autumn sowing in the open ground will achieve the same effect over the course of the winter. Some seeds require a much heavier dosage of cold and this can only be achieved by artificial storage at or below freezing point or by exposure to more than one winter's cold. Thus successful seed treatment to overcome this type of dormancy depends on:

(a) imbibed seeds
(b) adequate aeration
(c) 'cold' temperatures
(d) a period of time.

In order to avoid the use and maintenance of seedbeds for more than one season because of such a large cold requirement, the seeds can be stratified to break dormancy when artificial cold treatment is not available. The practical details of the process of stratification are dealt with in Appendix 3.2.

4.24 MULTIPLE DORMANCY

If the foregoing descriptions of dormancy always applied singly to particular plants, the overcoming of dormancy might not be quite the problem that it is in practice. Unfortunately many species complicate the picture by having developed combinations of different dormancy types. Thus in practice treatments to overcome these situations become more complex. The classic example is provided by the European Ash *(Fraxinus excelsior)* which has an immature embryo condition, this when matured still requires a conventional cold temperature to finally allow germination to occur and in stored dry seed, a hard seedcoat often develops. In this particular case straightforward stratification after winter collection provides a summer's warmth to provide maturation of the embryo and a winter's cold to complete the process. Similarly other types such as *Tilia* and *Carpinus* develop a hard seedcoat condition which however still require cold treatment of the imbibed seed when the seedcoat has been degraded, before germination can occur.

4.25 EPICOTYL DORMANCY

The phenomenon of double (epicotyl) dormancy is fortunately rather uncommon amongst woody subjects. It is typified by a type of germination, which in the season after sowing, allows only the radical to emerge and develop: the plumule does not emerge until the second season after a summer's warmth (because it is often immature) and a winter's cold (to break cold temperature controls). This condition provides in the practical situation a complex arrangement which requires occupation of the seedbed for two growing seasons. This unusual arrangement is commoner amongst herbaceous subjects — notably the *Liliaceae* — than woody subjects but appears in several north american species of Viburnums, *Smilax spp, Davidia* and the genus *Chionanthus,* on occasions it has also been noted in some samples of *Cedrus libani.*

23

4.26 SECONDARY DORMANCY

If a seed which is otherwise capable of germination by virtue of the normal inhibitions to germination having been removed, is subjected to unsuitable environmental conditions (especially high temperature) then a dormancy condition may redevelop often at very deep seated levels and require complex and concentrated treatment to overcome.

4.3 AVOIDING DORMANCY

As dormancy conditions can cause a number of vexing problems to the raiser of woody plants, and as they involve him in a number of extra and often complex procedures prior to the germination of a sample of seed, it may be prudent to determine whether it is possible to avoid the onset and development of dormancy factors within the seed, rather than have to overcome them subsequently.

In terms of the immature embryo condition it would normally require the season following dipersal to overcome dormancy, but if the seed is collected as soon as it can be removed from the parent and sown directly into a still warm seedbed in the late summer or early autumn, the embryo will be enabled to mature quickly because the seedcoat has not hardened, the seed can imbibe and the metabolic processes will continue. The subsequent winter cold will overcome any futher chilling requirement so that germination will occur in the first spring dispersal. This state of affairs accounts for the occasional references to Ash *(Fraxinus excelsior)* germinating in such a way after collection while still 'green'.

In many plants germination does not occur until the second spring after dispersal (and therefore necessitate stratification) because of the development of a sufficiently hard seedcoat which prevents imbibition and any necessary chilling treatment in the first winter (e.g. *Acer campestre, Viburnum lantana,* etc.)

The development of those factors causing dormancy or the inhibition of germination appear at a late stage in the maturation of the seed and are normally enhanced by the final drying phase prior to dispersal: indeed research has shown that germination inhibitors do not appear to any significant level in the seed until this stage of development is reached. If the seed could be collected as soon as the embryo has reached a mature size and the greater part of the food storage is complete, it should be capable of germination. If this stage is reached before any considerable dormancy factor (either hard seedcoat development or cold temperature requirement) is developed and occurs before the 'drying out' phase, then collection at this period coupled with the prevention of further drying should arrest any subsequent enhancement of the dormancy condition and allow germination after a normal winter's exposure to cold. This system has been evaluated and used so far for a limited range of subjects which include *Acer campestre, A. japonicum, A. pensylvanicum* and *Carpinus betulus.* An exactly similar technique can be employed for some fleshy or berried fruits, in this particular type the ripening flesh also, in many cases, produces an inhibitor which permeates the seed and enhances the dormancy condition. If, however, the seed is extracted from the unripe berry a comparable effect whereby the seedcoat is prevented from hardening and further permeation of the seed with inhibitor is prevented, the seed will germinate in the following spring: such a technique has been used for *Viburnum lantana, Hamamelis spp.* and *Daphne mezereum.* Similar effect in relation to hard seedcoats can be achieved if the fruits are collected at an early stage, and before drying, extracted and sown or kept moist thus preventing the hard seedcoat from developing and avoiding the necessity for a treatment to reduce the seedcoat.

This avoidance of dormancy, with the consequent saving both in time and treatment, has one useful side effect in that the seed also benefits from saving a year's food reserve which means a higher degree of germination vigour and large seedlings.

During the development of a seed after fertilisation of the ovule a number of discernible stages can be observed, these however merge as one stage begins before the completion of the previous stage.

Initially the cells divide to produce a foodstore and as this reaches adequate proportions it is used to provide the basic material for the development of the embryo which grows at its expense. Subsequently the conventional foodstores are differentiated and storage continues. As this stage reaches its final level the embryo matures to that stage at which it will be dispersed and become quiescent. The food store is then finally completed and the maturation of the seed and fruit coat begins, usually initially, by a reduction in moisture contents. During this phase dormancy controls develop as moisture content continues to decrease. Finally the seed or fruit matures to a stage suitable for dispersal and although the fruit many be succulent the seed is often characterised at this stage by being relatively dry.

At dispersal then the foodstore is complete, the embryo is quiescent and dormancy factors are developed. If dormancy is to be avoided then the external symptoms associated with the early stages of maturation of the seedcoat need to be recognised, so that the seed may be collected and kept moist in order to prevent any further maturation and the development of germination inhibitors.

This particular concept (the avoidance of dormancy) is not well researched and is operated empirically by a few propagators only. However, where mature seed bearing plants are available, and seed can be collected at that moment which is designated as desirable to achieve this effect, it has proved a useful method of avoiding the complexities of stratification or seedcoat treatment and the consequent difficulties in determining viability counts for seed rates. Often this particular condition is reached at a much earlier stage of development than might otherwise be expected — the best example being provided by *Daphne mezereum* which may be collected green in early June.

It may well, therefore, be worthwhile for a propagator to attempt to discern a suitable stage for collection rather than research, what is often unreliable, literature on temperatures and times required for stratification or other seed treatments. For the methods used in attempting to overcome dormancy conditions in seeds reflects the uncertainty concerning the dormancy conditions and combinations.

ASSOCIATED LITERATURE

Amen, R.D. (1968) 'A model of seed dormancy' Bot. Rev. *34*:1.

Barton, L.V. (1944) 'Some seeds showing special dormancy', Contrib. Boyce Thompson Inst. *13* (5):259.

Barton, L.V. (1947) 'Special Studies on seedcoat impermeability', Contrib. Boyce Thompson Inst. *14* (7): 355.

Barton, L.V. (1952) 'Dormancy in Seeds', Rep. 13th Int. hort. Congr.

Barton, L:V. (1961) Seed Preservation and Longevity', Leonard Hill.

Crocker, W. (1916) 'Mechanism of dormancy in seeds', Amer. J. Bot. *3*: 99.

Crocker, W., Thornton, N.W. and E.M. Schroeder (1946) 'Internal pressure necessary to break shells of nuts and the role of shells in delayed germination', Contrib. Boyce Thompson Inst. *14*(3): 1973.

Fordham, A.J. (1974) 'Dormancy in seeds of temperate woody plants', Proc. Int. Plant Prop. Soc. *23*: 262.

Frankland, B. and P.F. Wareing (1962) 'Changes in endogenous giberellins in relation to chilling of dormant seeds', Nature *194*: 313.

Hunter, J.B. and A.E. Erickson (1952) 'Relation of seed germination to moisture tension', Agron. Jour. *44:* 107.

Mayer, A.M. and A. Poljakoff-Mayber (1963) 'The Germination of Seeds', Macmillan, N.Y.

Nikolaeva, M.G. (1967) 'Physiology of Deep Dormancy in Seeds', Academy of Sciences of the U.S.S.R. translated by Israel Programme for Scientific Translation (1969), Jerusalem.

Pollock, B.M. and V.K. Toole (1961) 'After Ripening, rest period and dormancy', in 'Seeds', U.S.D.A. Yearb. Agric. :106.

Sarvas, R. (1950) 'The effect of light on the germination of forest tree seeds', Oikos *2*: 109.

Wareing, P.F. (1963) 'The germination of seeds', Vistas Bot. *3*: 195.

Wareing, P.F. and P.F. Saunders (1971) 'Hormones and Dormancy', Ann. Rev. Plant Phys. *22:* 261.

5 The Seedbed

The provision of an area for the successful production of seedlings would appear to be the most obvious of the horticultural factors involved in the system. However scant useful guidelines are available except in relation to the use of 'well drained sandy loams', the maintenance of 'good levels of humus', the choice of a 'protected' site and the 'general control of weeds' and similar conventional phraseology.

5.1 SITING THE SEEDBED

The positioning of the seedbed on the nursery will inevitably be limited by cropping policy and the location of utilities, but there are a number of factors which may influence the choice of site from the various available areas.

In order to promote the cropping of as large a grade of seedling as is possible within the time which is available, it is prudent to develop the longest possible growing season, which nevertheless must be compatible with the provision of the best possible growing conditions. It should be remembered that other factors are also involved in seedling growth which are not a function of the site *viz*: seed size, nutrition, pest and disease control, etc.

When dealing with ornamental subjects which will normally have a higher intrinsic value in comparison with forest tree production or the seedling production of hedging plants, it may prove worthwhile to invest greater capital in the enterprise in terms of site, shelter and soil amelioration than might otherwise be anticipated.

5.11 TEMPERATURE

When attempting to encourage as long and as an effective growing season as possible, the most obvious factor within the environment that will promote plant growth is the warmth of the site. The siting of the area in such a position that average ambient temperatures will be higher than surrounding areas, will provide a condition for earlier and more rapid genermination, faster seedling growth and an overall longer growing season.

Siting on a southerly aspect will encourage an earlier increase in soil temperature in the spring and higher temperatures throughout the season. However, temperature is not only an effect of aspect but will also be governed by shelter and the incidence of radiation frost, demonstrating that environmental factors cannot be considered in isolation.

5.12 FROST INCIDENCE

If, by satisfactory siting, the growing season is advanced to induce earlier germination and seedling emergence, the seedling will be at risk over longer period to the incidence of radiation frost. Considerations related to the choice of site must therefore initially assess the statistical incidence of such frosts in the area in terms of the probable risk. Secondly the risk should be assessed in terms of local topography and the site should allow for adequate air drainage so that the actual occurrence of frost over the seedbed is reduced to a minimum. Attention should also be given to the provisions made for shelter so that cold air drainage is not impeded.

5.13 LIGHT

The recommendation to site the area with a southerly aspect with its implication of increased temperature, also implies that the site will have good light characteristics, unless the shelter causes much obscuring of incoming radiation.

The importance of light is necessarily in relation to the promotion of the photosynthetic processes and the provision in consequence of adaquate carbohydrates for active growth.

5.14 SHELTER

Probably the least recognised factor in the microclimate of the seedbed is the effect of wind. It is usually the most under-estimated, single, deleterious agency in the environment of the seedbed.

The effect of wind on seedling growth by causing physical damage to leaves, water loss from the plant and temperature reduction is very often completely overlooked. Exposure to even apparently innocuous wind speeds — as occur in so called summer breezes — markedly influences the rate of seedling growth. A measurement of several *Acer* species (a genus particularly susceptible to the efforts of wind) indicated a doubling in the size of the seedling by the end of the growing season when protected by 50% mesh screen on an open site.

5.15 DRAINAGE

Although it would be impractical to consider establishing a seed nursery on a badly drained site, consideration must nevertheless be given to ensuring that basic field drainage is adequate to take away excess water which may result from extended periods of irrigation through the growing season or snow melt which is likely to occur at a critical period in the germination phase of the crop.

As the encouragement of good root development is an essential feature of successful and vigorous seedling production, all drainage systems must be very satisfactory if adequate aeration of soil is to be maintained.

5.2 COMPOSITION OF THE SEEDBED

The composition of the seedbed will of necessity be based, at least from a consideration of cost, on the naturally occurring mineral soil of the nursery. The production of a completely artificial seedbed such as that envisaged for the Dunemann technique is too expensive an input, even for the majority of ornamental subjects under normal circumstances.

Ideally a light sandy loam would provide a good basis for a seed nursery but as most nurseries are already sited by other considerations it is necessary to consider the improvement of a soil which may not be the most desirable.

How much amelioration will be necessary depends on the condition of the soil at the start, but with few exceptions most nursery soils will benefit from the incorporation of fairly massive applications of bulky organic matter in order to promote the long term improvement of soil structure. As this may prove expensive in terms of farmyard manure, spent hops, etc. a series of quick developing green crops will effectively achieve the same end product. A final topping up with coarse peat, spent hops or leaf mould may then prove reasonably economical.

If the soil is of a heavy texture it may also prove beneficial to incorporate grit to assist with drainage.

All these improvements are aimed at ameliorating soil condition so that it approaches that ideal balance between drainage, aeration and water retention.

However, the principles and benefits of the Dunemann system should not be overlooked, as the technique provides a number of relevant pointers towards improved seedling production. The incorporation of leaf mould, in as large a quantity as is available, will induce one of the major benefits of the system — that is the provision of mycorrhizal associations. Although the technique was devised for coniferous subjects these associations, in some degree, are also an essential feature of many woody broad leaved subjects. Even those subjects which are not dependent on a mycorrhiza forming appear to produce a more fibrous seedling root system than would normally be expected from a conventional mineral soil seedbed under these conditions.

No generalised seedbed composition will be ideal or even suitable for all subjects but the above description describes a condition suitable for the satisfactory germination of the great majority. Exceptions which will require special conditions will only be discovered with experience.

5.21 SOIL REACTION

The basic reaction of the soil has some significance in the production of seedlings, and in altering the composition of the seedbed by the addition of various materials, the reaction of the finished area will in all probability have been significantly altered. It may therefore be reasonable to attempt to manipulate this factor by judicious use of those additional materials which are used in altering the composition. Successive green cropping will require the application of nitrogen between crops in order to avoid starvation in the next crop; the pH could be influenced by the use of either nitro-chalk or sulphate of ammonia (an acid salt) as the nitrogen additive. The choice of spent hops, coarse peat or leaf mould, could also materially alter reaction.

It would appear that as a general rule coniferous subjects and most ericaceous type plants require a seedbed reaction of between 4.5 and 5.5 while most others succeed in the range 5.5 to 6.5.

5.3 NUTRITION

The nutrition of tree and shrub seedbeds is a relatively unresearched area although some evidence has been accumulated for forest tree nurseries and some guidelines have been developed.

Ornamental woody plants do not appear to exhibit any particular differences in their consumption and requirements of nutrients when compared with other more conventional crops. In common with almost all other crops they require a balanced supply of the normally expected elements. No one element can be cited as being more important than any other; as a shortage of any one, despite all the others being readily available, will dramatically affect plant growth. The important consideration is therefore to ensure that the nutrient status of the seedbed is continually monitored by at least an annual analysis, so that corrections by the addition of suitable fertilisers can be effected in order to achieve a base level.

Under normal circumstances it is only necessary to apply suitable compounds of Nitrogen, Potassium and Phosphorus regularly, while on less regular occasions Magnesium may be limiting and this situation will need rectifying. It is unlikely under normal nursery practices that any other element will become deficient, as the impurities in the normal fertilisers used will maintain the level of secondary elements such as calcium and sulphur and minor elements such as Iron, Manganese, Boron, etc. at a satisfactory level.

It is necessary to assess the nutrient status each year before sowing so that determined base levels of nutrients will allow a return to these figure. This will entail in the first instance a soil analysis on an accurate basis.

In the annual preparation of the seedbed it is only worth applying those elements which are less easily leached from the soil. Nitrogen and Potassium are usually very soluble and in consequence there is little point in applying any appreciable quantities of their salts until they are required. Phosphorus is less mobile in the soil and is also significant in the base dressing stage because of its early importance to the germinating seed; its role is chiefly in energy relationships and as a structural component of important nucleic proteins. This should not preclude the addition of Nitrogen and Potassium but as their role in plant growth is largely important after emergence only a lower level is necessary in the base dressing. They can more effectively be applied in small but regular top dressing applications during the growing season.

Some consideration must also be given to the levels of Magnesium as with the annual removal of so much plant growth and leaves the level of this element can quickly diminish.

5.31 FERTILISER MATERIALS

The type of compound employed in the application of these nutrients is also of some significance both in relation to their affect upon pH and on the rate at which they become available to the crop. Although relatively expensive, the modern development of slow release fertilisers may take much of the uncertainty out of the questions of how much to apply and in the case of top dressings — when? Traditionally many agricultural type fertilisers have been used on seedbeds such as 'Nitro Chalk' and Muriate of Potash — both of which can have considerable influence on pH levels.

For quick action Ammonium nitrate and Potassium nitrate are most effective and are easily applied in solution.

Magnesium Limestone provides a suitable vehicle for increasing pH as well as improving Magnesium levels, while if only the latter is necessary Epsom salts will be more accurate and speedy.

5.4 STERILISATION OF SEEDBEDS

The subject of soil sterilisation in relation to seedbeds is a difficult subject on which to be dogmatic, for the exercise highlights a number of effects which may conflict with each other when considering benefits to the seedling.

If the seedbed were infested with a particular pest or infected with a disease causing organism, then sterilisation would have obvious advantages in the terms of avoiding crop losses. This would prove to be specifically important with reference to the control of Potato Cyst Eelworm and the presently accepted E.E.C. regulations governing the movement of plants grown on soil with infestations above the accepted minimum.

The control of weeds should not provide a necessary reason for sterilising, as good husbandry techniques should not allow the build up of weed populations to such a level that they require this type of treatment.

One of the side effects of some types of soil sterilisation which is of benefit to the crop is the enhanced rate of seedling growth obtained following treatment, this is often of a greater magnitude than can be accounted for by the removal of competition provided by weeds and pathogens. This effect has been attributed to an increase in ammonium — nitrogen liberated by the treatment but investigations have not proved conclusive. However it cannot be denied that often such a benefit accrues after sterilisation and this phenomenon should not be disallowed when assessing its value.

Probably the most important disadvantage of sterilising the seedbed is the inevitable reduction in the non-pathogenic fungi which are eliminated. In some cases these have been introduced laboriously by the incorporation of leaf mould, so that suitable fungal associations are immediately available to the emerging radicle and a mycorrhiza can immediately and effectively develop. For those subjects which are heavily dependent on this type of association, seedbed sterilisation could be disastrous. However, recent opinion suggests that 'spore rain' is so universal that sterilised seedbeds are quickly re-inoculated although mycorrhizal association at an effective level may be delayed.

The range of materials available for seedbed sterilisation which are effective on the highly organic anthropomorphic soils, which are eventually produced in seedbeds, are fairly limited. Forest tree nurseries have made extensive use of formalin soaks very successfully. 'Dazomet' has proved effective in horticultural sterilisation and is fairly easy to use. Methyl bromide is also successful but is a lethal chemical and requires treatment by a licensed operator. Allyl alcohol also falls into this category.

5.41 WEED CONTROL

The elimination of perennial weeds is of the utmost importance in the preparation of the seedbed. Such weeds are notoriously difficult to eradicate once the crop is growing and they are capable of considerable reduction in crop yields at even moderate levels of infestation. If the land is adequately cultivated it is unlikely that a very large population will remain and what is left can be spot treated with suitable herbicides or physically forked out.

The problem of annual weeds is relatively easily overcome by fallowing that proportion of the area which is required for autumn sowing. The weeds beings controlled by the cultivations required for preparation of the beds throughout the season. Once the seedbed has been completed and the final stages of preparation are being undertaken during the summer, weed seeds in the surface layers can be eliminated by using the 'stale seedbed' technique — this involves the preparation of the seedbeds as if for sowing and then spraying out seedlings with a suitable contact herbicide as they emerge.

The control of weeds after the crop has germinated should thus be virtually eliminated. However wind blown seeds, etc. will inevitably appear but these can be controlled by hand until the crop makes enough leaf cover to smother weeds.

5.5 PREPARATION OF THE SEEDBED

Seedbed preparation involves developing those conditions in the soil which will encourage the best root system and allow the most ready availability of water and nutrients.

It also implies the elimination of perennial weeds, the reasonable control of annual weed populations and the satisfactory control of harmful soil borne organisms.

The difficulty in seedbed preparation is attempting to balance the requirement of reasonable moisture retention and an acceptable degree of aeration without too rapid or excessive drying and the consequent development of water stress.

This ideal can only be achieved by a balanced system of materials being incorporated with the normal soil to produce a composition which develops a well structured condition.

Probably the most important feature in the preparation of the seedbed is the development of adequate drainage, as successful germination will depend ultimately on good aeration. However, germination cannot proceed without water, so water retention at a sufficiently low tension is also of paramount significance.

The development of a good structure is therefore essential. Drainage can be improved by raising the beds either by 'throwing up' the beds from the paths or by improving more permanently raised beds. If the seedbeds are thrown up from paths it will entail the preparation of the entire area and the economics of this phase will be governed by the seedbed to path ratio. If the beds have a more permanent edging then amelioration is limited to the bed areas although mechanisation may not be so efficient.

When all the additions have been made to the seedbed area, it is then worked to a uniform composition so that variations in production due to this aspect can be reduced to a minimum. Further preparations prior to sowing must also produce uniform effects.

One of the chief difficulties in throwing up beds, which is normally carried out with two potato ridging bodies and a levelling board, is that the soil from the paths is only thrown onto the edges of the bed and tends to cause greater consolidation in these areas unless the levelling equipment is designed to overcome this factor.

After working to this stage the soil should be light and friable and will require levelling and some compaction. However, the chief reason postulated for heavy compaction is to allow capillary rise of water but if adequate provision of irrigation facilities is available this is less significant and greater aeration can be allowed for by less compaction.

When the seedbed has been uniformly worked, levelled and compacted it is prepared as for sowing, i.e. irrigated and finely levelled. This causes the weed seeds to germinate which can then be sprayed out with a suitable contact herbicide. Repeated successive use of this technique soon reduces annual weed seed populations.

After this treatment the seedbed is ready for sowing once it has been irrigated and brought to field capacity.

Although this aspect of production must appear to be a simple and commonsense procedure, the attention to detail and the development of uniform conditions is nevertheless the essence of success for the production of an even batch of seedlings. Hasty and skimped preparation results in an uneven seedbed which varies in its compaction, drainage, aeration and composition, with its consequent variable effects on the seedling population throughout the growing season.

ASSOCIATED READING

'Windbreaks for Orchards', M.A.F.F., S.T.L. *104* (1972).
'Shelter Hedges and Trees', M.A.F.F., Rosewarne E.H.S., Sta. Lflt. *2* (1970).
'Shelter Belts and Microclimate', For. Comm. Bull. *29,* H.M.S.O. (1957).
'Shelter Belts and Windbreaks', J.M. Caborn, Faber and Faber (1966).
'Experiments on nutrition problems in forest nurseries', For. Comm. Bull. *37,* H.M.S.O. (1965), 2 Vols.

6 Sowing the Seed

The main objective in any commercial system of seedling production must essentially be to achieve a realistic level of productivity from the seedbed, and if the seedbed is to be used to maximum effect it must be exploited economically. This requires the production of the greatest number of seedlings of a minimum predetermined quality from a given area. Quality in this instance will imply, for the greater part, a particular size or grade relevant to an individual subject.

This later assessment is usually derived in terms of a measurement of the height of the seedling or stem circumference of the seedling, and is in the final analysis a function of the density of the seedling population. In any one season however, this is very much dependent on the assumption that the quality of the seedbed and the level of husbandry are maintained at a constant and acceptable standard from year to year.

Assuming then a standard level of husbandry, the grade (i.e. quality) of the seedlings produced will be a function of the plant population and initially therefore it is necessary to assess the maximum density at which this required quality can be achieved.

Unfortunately the availability of this type of information is very limited and although much very effective work has produced useful results for forestry practice, it has little relevance to the production of high quality, high value, ornamental woody plant seedlings on a relatively small scale. Usually this knowledge is only available from the experience gained under particular local conditions. In most circumstances it would be unwise to attempt exact specifications for seedling populations because of the considerable variations that occur in local conditions and the required end product, although some indications of reasonable population ranges for a particular subject must be made in order to provide an initial base from which the propagator can begin to develop his own experience.

6.1 ASSESSMENT OF SEEDING RATE

Having predetermined husbandry levels and the expected quality of the seedlings then the plant population of any particular subject also becomes fixed. Hence in the assessment of how much seed to sow, this population target figure is the principal factor involved and the success of this particular part of the exercise will be limited by the accuracy with which it is achieved and the various losses and limitations to growth between the actual sowing of the seed and the harvesting of the final seedling stand can be assessed.

The amount of seed to be sown to achieve a particular seedling stand will then be calculated from the following information:—

    (a) the required seedling population
    (b) the viability of the seed sample
    (c) the purity of the seed sample
    (d) the field factor
    (e) the seed count for the sample.

6.11 CALCULATION OF THE SOWING RATE

When producing trees and shrubs from seed in an open ground seedbed the critical features determining the successful production of the size and quality of the seedling crop are the population of seedlings in the seedbed and the level of husbandry which the crop receives.

The object in growing a crop of seedlings should be to achieve a particular grade for a specified purpose: and if it is assumed that a standard level of husbandry is practiced and maintained from year to year then the size of each individual seedling within the crop will be governed by the degree of competition provided between these individual plants. Thus individual size reflects the amount of space available to each seedling. The density at which the crop is grown must therefore be one of the most important assessments to be made.

Only experience of one's own local climate, seedbeds and husbandry standards will determine at what density the seedlings will need to be grown to achieve a particular size and quality; and it is this aspect of production which requires the first series of observational exercises. In the first year or so seedling crops should be grown at slightly varying densities on either side of the anticipated population so that an assessment can be made under local conditions. These varying populations can be achieved by either sowing at varying seed rates or by sowing an area at the highest density and thinning to the required populations.

The prime function of the exercise then is to sow seeds at a particular calculated rate such that the required ideal population of seedlings is achieved. Incorrect assessments of the various components involved in the calculation will result in either too few seedlings of too great size or too many undersized seedlings. At least with the latter of these problems it is feasible to thin the crop; so that it is probably better to err on under-estimating rather than end up with an uneconomically sparse crop.

The calculation of the seed-rate to achieve a particular population of seedlings is a relatively simple arithmetical exercise and in various forms has been used by field scale vegetable growers for many years. It does however, for its success, depend on making certain assessments for each individual seed lot with some accuracy.

In general principle the calculation in each of its elementary features consists of modifying the seedling density by a series of factors so that it is converted to a quantity of seed which when sown will produce that density of seedlings.   35

In simplest terms — we do not normally expect to sow 'X' seeds to produce 'X' seedlings, because we know that a certain proportion of the seeds are dead, so this factor increases the number of seeds in order to compensate. It is also well known that, for various reasons, not all the live seeds will germinate and develop as established seedlings, so that the seed number must be modified again accordingly to account for this: it is then necessary to convert this number to a weight by carrying out a simple count.

Thus the sowing rate is calculated from the following information:—

(i)   **The Plant Population:** i.e. the density at which the seedling crop is to be grown to reach the required standard and grade by the end of the season. This fundamental aspect will depend on each individual species and its reaction to a particular site, the preparation of the seedbed and the degree of sophistication of husbandry technique to which it is subjected. The plant population is most readily expressed in seedlings/m^2.

(ii)   **The Viability of the Seed:** this is a measure of the number of live seeds within a seed sample; it should be measured just prior to sowing so that further losses will not be sustained during any subsequent storage. The figure can be assessed by a cutting test if the seed is large enough to observe easily; a germination test if no dormancy controls are present or by a Tetrazolium Test if dormancy conditions are a problem. Viability is usually expressed as a percentage live seeds in the sample.

(iii)   **The Field Factor:** is a conglomerate assessment of all those factors which may prevent some of the viable seeds within the sample from germinating and/or establishing themselves as seedlings.

This is necessarily a subjective judgement and should take account of such considerations as seed size (ability to survive), seed vigour, seedbed conditions, season of sowing (survival period before germination occurs), season of emergence, incidence of 'damping off' diseases etc. All these factors and their interactions must be weighed in the light of experience so that the proportion of seeds likely to survive to establishment as seedlings can be assessed. The vegetable grower usually expresses this figure as decimal fraction (e.g. 0.8) but for this purpose it is as easily represented as a percentage.

(iv)   **The Count:** represents the number of seeds per unit weight at the time of sowing. This assessment simply converts number into weight. This quantity is normally expressed as a figure/kg. This is also a relevant figure to have generally available as it gives an indication of quantities, if seeds have to be bought in, rather than collected locally.

The calculation of the sowing rate is derived from the following formula:—

$$\text{Seed Rate} = \frac{\text{Plant Population}}{\text{Viability x Field Factor x Count}}$$

Example

Norway Maple *(Acer platanoides)* collected 'green' and sown without undue delay provided the following detail:—

(i) Plant population required to produce 6 - 10mm grade, 1 year
seedlings 140/m²
(ii) Viability by a cutting test and visual observation 80%
(iii) Field Factor (autumn sowing; large, good quality seed; good
seedbed conditions) 70%
(iv) Seed count 4,000/kg

Therefore seed rate $= 140 \times \dfrac{100}{80} \times \dfrac{100}{70} \times \dfrac{1}{4,000}$

$= 62.5 \text{ gm/m}^2$

This figure now needs to be multiplied by the area of seedbed to be occupied by the crop to give the total amount of seed to be sown.

However this can only be calculated once the total crop requirements have been ascertained.

A further simple calculation is required but this must take account of the fact that it is not likely, even if the desired plant population is attained, that a full (100%) grade out will be achieved. It is therefore necessary to estimate, from experience, what proportion of the crop will actually grade out at the required quality. If all other factors are equal this is most likely to be a function of seed provenance: hence it will require an initial screening of various source trees to assess which parent trees provide the most consistent results. If seedling husbandry is consistent and uniform then this should be a limiting factor.

EXAMPLE

— continuing the previous calculation *(Acer platanoides)*, given:—

(a) Required total crop of grade 10,000
(b) Grade out of 6 - 10mm 100/m²

then **Total area required** $= \dfrac{10,000}{100}$ $= 100\text{m}^2$

given:—

(a) Seed rate 62.5gm/m²

then **Total seed requirement** $= 100 \times 62.5$
$= 6.25 \text{ kg}$

It will be seen that the calculations required are not difficult, but they are of paramount significance in producing a seedling crop of a pre-determined quality: and for ultimate success depend on the accurate understanding of all the factors involved.

6.2 SEASONS OF SOWING

The question of when to sow seed is relatively easy to answer but is inevitably qualified because of imponderables and variables. Seeds with transient vitality such as Poplars, Willows and some Elms must be sown immediately on dispersal, as they have poorly developed seedcoats and the seeds are very susceptible to dessication which makes them difficult to store without specialised equipment.

Those subjects producing seed in the early summer such as *Acer rubrum, Acer saccharinum* and *Betula nigra* have fairly short longevity and must therefore be sown straight away when they will quickly germinate and establish.

If fresh seed can be obtained then there is a continuous succession of subjects to be sown throughout the summer months and although germination does not occur till the following spring this period in warm moist conditions aids the decomposition of limited hard seedcoats, allows embryo maturation and the full imbibition of the seed prior to the winter chilling.

Early autumn begins a busy season for sowing, large seeded subjects being sown immediately on dispersal and many Maples and such subjects as Hornbeam being collected and sown 'green' to avoid two year dormancy. The sowing of subjects requiring winter chilling before germination will also occur at this period.

Winter sowing is usually concerned with stratified seed which has been treated for the previous twelve months. The seed is sown in early to mid winter in order to provide an even penetration of winter cold to the seed and also because many subjects such as *Crataegus* and *Fraxinus excelsior* chit very early in storage and do not survive sowing satisfactorily in this condition.

Spring sowing is normally carried out with those subjects, such as most leguminous species which do not require winter chilling: and the majority of conifers, which are usually sown late to avoid too excessive an exposure to radiation frost in the early seedling stage.

6.3 METHOD OF SOWING

Once the seedbed has been irrigated and brought to field capacity it can be finally levelled for sowing.

The seed is then distributed at the calculated rate taking care to ensure that sowing is even and correct by check sampling. This requires a windless day for absolute success. The seed is broadcast in order to achieve an evenly distributed population and uniform seedling development. Sowing in rows often tends to produce a higher proportion of culls and a greater variation in size due to the increased competition and 'side' effects.

After sowing the seed is lightly rolled or pressed into the seedbed in order to encourage good contact (for moisture uptake) with the soil. The bed is then covered with a layer of coarse grit (3-5 mm clear) up to 15 mm thick. This latter less conventional aspect of the technique provides for (i) the even percolation of precipitation, (ii) the maintenance of an open compost surface and well aerated conditions around the seed, (iii) facilitates the removal of wind blown weed seedlings, (iv) the elimination of capping and splashing, (v) the prevention of colonisation by moss and liverworts and (vi) an adequate barrier to discourage the establishment of weak seedlings.

Although it appears to be simple on paper to describe seed sowing a number of practical problems emerge with experience. The distribution of small seed is often difficult to effect evenly but this can be achieved by extending the seed with an inert material, however the particle size must be similar otherwise the seed will not permeate evenly. Some seeds have a particularly neutral colour which makes them difficult to distinguish from the background colour of the seedbed and to distribute these evenly it may be advantageous to colour them, either with a seed dressing if it is relevant or with a dye. Sowing stratified seed is not always easy, in most cases the seed and stratifying medium are sown together after ensuring that all is evenly mixed, however, if for any reason the seed has to be sown without the medium it is necessary to ensure that the particle size of the medium is distinct from that of the seed so that it can be successfully screened out.

In the process of hand sowing across a wide (in excess of 1.5 m) seedbed it may assist even distribution to employ a cuffing board, this is held upright on the far side of the bed to cause any seed projected too vigorously to bounce back into the bed. This practice is well established on forest tree nurseries.

When selecting a grit for covering the seed, size of particle is relevant but more importantly it should be lime free so that the reaction of the seedbed is not altered; and silt free so that the seed is not smothered by sedimenting silt. In practical terms the seed is rolled in and then covered with grit, it is important that the grit is distributed low over the seed to avoid bouncing the seed and taking it out of contact from the seedbed. With winged seeds which are particularly liable to bounce the effect can be reduced by watering before covering.

Before sowing it may be prudent to dress the seed with a tainting substance such as Red Lead or Paraffin if rodents are a problem, or with a suitable fungicide if 'Damping Off' diseases are prevalent.

ASSOCIATED READING

Heit, C.E. (1967 a) 'Propagation from Seed 5: Control of seedling density', Amer.Nurs. *125* (8): 14.

Heit, C.E. (1967 b) 'Propagation from Seed 9: Fall sowing of conifer seed', Amer. Nurs. *126*(6): 10.

Heit, C.E. (1968) 'Propagation from Seed 15: Fall planting of shrub seeds for successful seedling production', Amer. Nurs. *128*(4): 8.

7 Seedling Husbandry

The satisfactory production of an economic crop of seedlings not only depends on an assessment of the various factors involved in persuading the seed to germinate and then establish as a seedling, but that it subsequently grows and attains the size and grade envisaged.

Whether or not a satisfactory crop is produced is then a function of the maintenance of a particular level of husbandry performance. Such standards must be set and adhered to, as the calculation determining seed rates is very much dependent on a specific level of husbandry at a particular plant population, so that seedlings of the grade required will be reached by the end of the growing season.

If it is assumed that the seedbed has been satisfactorily prepared and is even and uniform in its characteristics, then the production of the required crop is only dependent on husbandry performance.

Successful husbandry is dependent on limiting any restriction to plant growth to a reasonable and practical minimum. In practice the availability of water and plant nutrients, limited control of the microclimate, the protection of the crop from pests and diseases and the elimination of weed competition are the most obvious agencies which will materially check seedling growth and development.

7.1 PREVENTION OF WATER STRESS

The production of the crop will, *inter alia,* be very much dependent on the availability of sufficient water for plant growth. The growth of the seedlings is very much affected by water and the subjection of the crop to any severe degree of water stress will reduce the rate of growth materially. Although there is virtually no evidence to indicate the levels of water stress which woody plant seedlings will withstand without any obvious check to growth, it is reasonable to suppose that they will not differ greatly from other types of plants. Vegetable crops, for instance, have been shown to thrive best if the moisture deficit is kept to the minimum level which practicalities will allow. The regular application of relatively small quantities of water to maintain the seedbed as near Field Capacity as is feasible has proved beneficial and successful under conditions of continental climate. However some form of monitoring the moisture deficit will prove more useful under the variable conditions of a maritime climate, as water need only be applied in sufficient

40

quantity once a particular level of tension has been reached. As weather conditions may vary considerably, a 'regular' application either may not be sufficient and cause stress or may be excessive and induce some leaching. The use of a simple, porous pot type, soil moisture tensiometer gives a continuous and sufficiently accurate indication of soil moisture conditions so that water can be applied in adequate quantities with reasonable accuracy. From those observations which are available it would appear that seedlings of woody plants will experience a noticeable check to growth at about a two inch soil moisture deficit.

The actual application of water does not present a problem as the types of irrigation equipment available nowadays is sufficiently varied that equipment with a suitable spread pattern and rate of application can readily be selected for almost any requirement. The availability of a source of water, however, may be a problem if irrigation is not already an established practice on the nursery.

Some attention should also be paid to the reaction and content of the water. Water with a high pH may cause quite large alterations to the reaction of a seedbed over the course of a season, increases 1 to 1½ units have been recorded. The source of the water should also be regularly monitored for any materials which may be detrimental to the growth of the crop. River water should be checked for detergent levels and other pollutant materials. Artesian well water would appear harmless but on occasions has proved to be dangerously high in various salts, causing a servere scorch of seedlings. The source of water should therefore be analysed initially, and then screened at regular intervals to provide a check against the occurrance of untoward pollutants which may cause checks to seedling growth.

7.2 THE NUTRITION OF SEEDLINGS

The successful control and regulation of the availability of plant nutrients is one of the most difficult aspects of seedling crop husbandry. The influence of the climate with its continual and unpredictable variations in this country make the assessment of nutrient levels uncertain without the availability of specialised analytical equipment or an expensive laboratory service. The maintenance of a balanced supply of nutrients is normally based on the annual analysis which has been determined at the time of seedbed preparation and by experience of subsequent climatic conditions which determine such factors as crop growth, rate of leaching etc. Long lasting nutrients are conventionally supplied in the base dressing and quickly leached elements are kept to a satisfactory level by liquid feeding or top dressing during the growing season.

The base dressing applied in the preparation of the seedbed will usually satisfy the annual requirement of phosphate and magnesium, although further additions in the second half of the growing season may be marginally necessary. However, nitrogen and potash are highly soluble and are not required at the germination stage of the seedling crop in any large quantities until its establishment as a green plant. The application of these elements in the base dressing has to be in slow acting organic form if their availability is to last past germination without loss by leaching, hence it is more satisfactory and cheaper to apply these nutrients during the growing season.

41

Methods of application during the growing season offer two alternatives. Conventionally fertiliser has been added as a solid, highly soluble, crystalline or granular material which is effective for quick action. This type of application may cause scorch if, in distribution, the solid settles on the plant itself, especially in hot weather. Continental experience suggests that liquid feeding at low concentrations at regular intervals minimises most of the problems as it avoids scorch etc., and encourages continuous growth without any nutritional limitation throughout the season. It also prevents the sudden build up of salt concentrations in the seedbed but this technique however only works well if it is coupled with an adequate irrigation system.

Seedling growth will, of course, depend on a variety of other elements being available. Many of these will be supplied in sufficient quantities as impurities in agricultural grade fertilisers and in organic base dressings when used.

Sulphur is normally never limiting because of the extensive use of sulphates as fertiliser materials. Calcium is rarely in short supply because liming the seedbeds will be necessary for correction of pH even if it is only infrequently.

Minor or trace elements become in short supply if pure material (such as Nitrate of Potash and Urea) are used in the formulation of liquid feeds, and similar inorganic materials are used in base dressings. Normally they occur as impurities. Such shortages can be overcome by the use of fritted trace elements when analysis indicates a problem, and as a matter of policy it may be wise to maintain subclinical applications to prevent such a situation occuring.

7.21 TIMING OF FERTILISER APPLICATION

In general it would appear that the greatest benefits are achieved by the regular application of small quantities of nutrients throughout the season. However, modern slow release materials such as the 'Enmag' types means that only two applications of solid top dressings may be necessary in a season.

How long into the late season these nutrients should be applied is an uncertain question as evidence is conflicting. Continued used of nitrogen into the autumn may well delay normal leaf fall because of continued growth and so increase the level of damage caused by radiation frost because of the delaying of wood maturation. However, if high levels of potash are maintained this appears to partially mitigate against this effect. This suggests that at the beginning of the season a relatively high nitrogen, low potash balance is more useful and that gradually throughout the season these levels are reversed.

7.22 MINOR ELEMENT TOXICITY

It would not be prudent to pass over the question of nutrition without indicating that the possibility, of toxic, minor element conditions developing, does exist. These chiefly arise as high concentrations of heavy metal ions if sewage manures derived from urban industrial situations have been used in order to bulk the organic matter content of the seedbed. Zinc has several times proved troublesome under this type of condition.

7.3 MANIPULATION OF THE SEEDBED MICROCLIMATE

Although the outdoor production of woody plant seedlings does not, by its nature, permit a great deal of environmental control, certain aspects of the microclimate of the area can be influenced for the benefit of crop growth with a consequent general improvement in quality.

7.31 WIND AND THE PROVISION OF SHELTER

It has already been indicated in the remarks concerned with the siting of seedbeds that the deleterious effect of wind on seedling growth is perhaps the most dramatically demonstrable of all environmental factors affecting seedling growth. Wind not only promotes the development of water stress within the seedling but it is also an important contributor to the reduction of the ambient temperature. An increase in wind speed also causes a marked increase of mechanical damage in such closely spaced crops, with the consequent reduction in photosynthetic area and potential carbohydrate loss. All these effects will produce a marked reduction in crop growth even at the modest wind speeds experienced during most of the growing season. The provision of peripheral shelter and windbreaking is a factor to be considered when siting and establishing a seedbed area, however the use of shelter internally to provide localised protection is likely to be less permanent and should be considered as a husbandry technique.

The provision of temporary shelter using artificial materials such as netting, wood laths and plastic mesh to filter wind must be considered and this should provide approximately a 50 per cent permeability. Lower filtering effects or solid barriers tend to develop eddying effects on both windward and leeward sides and at high windspeeds can cause considerable damage to the crop.

7.32 RADIATION FROST

The incidence of radiation frosts and their severity both at the beginning and at the end of the season presents a very real problem to effective seedling production. For it is this factor which effectively governs the length of the growing season rather than the onset or cessation of ambient temperatures of sufficient magnitude to produce plant growth. The regular occurrence of radiation frost in the early season may depress soil temperatures sufficiently to delay germination, while their incidence however irregular after the period of germination may severely check growth, or at the worst, cause the death of the crop.

Thus the available weather statistics should be surveyed to ascertain not only the regularity of such frosts throughout the season but also their severity, which may proportionately affect the degree of damage. This information will then provide a basis for determining the type and cost of protection to be afforded on a particular site.

The information in itself provides, regrettably, only a partial guide, as the level of damage caused by a frost on a particular date in late spring or early summer will depend on the date of emergence of each subject and its own relative hardiness in withstanding frost. These factors will also be determined by the previous weather conditions; for an early spring will obviously induce greater susceptibilities to otherwise conventional seasons of frost incidence — as was well demonstrated by the 1945 season when a very early spring induced early growth which was then decimated by an otherwise normal frost in late April; while the 1935 season was typified by continuous and severe mid May frosts which caused damage in an otherwise normal season.

So many factors are however bound up in causing the severity of frost damage and the picture is further complicated by the rate of thaw, the humidity of the atmosphere etc., that reference should be made to relevant literature if it is proposed to site a seedbed in an area notorious for the occurrence of radiation frosts.

During the spring period seedlings, in general, are very susceptible to cold temperature damage; under natural circumstances in the thicket, hedgerow or forest, the seedling is protected by the existing plant canopy against the penetration of radiation frost. In an open ground seedbed situation it is necessary to take positive, protective action to compensate for this factor if growth is not to be checked or death occur.

Autumn radiation frosts may cause widespread damage as seedlings will not usually have developed full winter hardiness, and the problem can be further compounded by high nitrogen feeding during the late summer which causes late extension growth. For this reason in areas which may be prone to such frosts, it is important to harden the crop at an early stage by decreasing nitrogen feeding, reducing water applications and increasing potash feeding.

Frost protection is achieved most simply by placing a layer of evergreen coniferous branches above the seedlings, so it is this surface which radiates. Alternatively the same effect can be achieved by covering the beds with laths or suspending matting or plastic mesh over the beds. This involves the provision of some superstructure, albeit cheap, to provide support and keep the material off the seedlings. On a large scale these materials may simply prove too tiresome and bulky to handle and some simpler protection must be devised.

Effective frost protection can be achieved by the judicious and timely use of irrigation on exactly the same lines as that practiced by the soft fruit producers who wish to protect their blossom against frost. The success of the technique depends on coating the radiating surfaces with water just prior to the onset of freezing temperatures so that protection is effected by the loss of heat from the water and eventually by the latent heat as the water turns to ice. In order to be fully of value the protective water film must be maintained throughout the period of freezing so that ice is continually formed on the already frozen surfaces.

Cold temperature in the early summer period can make quite disastrous checks to growth in the seedlings of many subjects. Although it is clearly impossible to legislate for unseasonable weather, the statistical likelihood of such incidence should be determined when assessing a particular site for seedbed production. Thus on any particular site, precautions to prevent undue loss and the amelioration of site conditions where possible to reduce incidence will help in cushioning the effect.

7.33 SHADE

Many woody subjects will normally germinate under shade conditions provided by the canopy of mature vegetation and it may not be unreasonable to suppose that they require such conditions in the seedbed. However, experience indicates that the greater proportion of species benefits from exposure to normal light conditions with the consequent increased photosynthetic activity.

Experience in the British Isles suggests that only very few subjects materially benefit from shade in the seedbed, basically the climate is cool and moist, and shading under these conditions will normally reduce photosynthetic activity during most of the growing season as well as producing drawn, spindly plants. Shade should therefore be used with caution and sparingly. It is conventional practice to recommend shading for a number of coniferous subjects especially *(e.g. Abies, Picea* and *Pseudotsuga)* but during a normal summer in these islands the number of days when light intensity reaches a sufficient level to cause a check to growth are few and does not compensate for the overall loss sustained by the continued depression of available light for photosynthesis produced by the shading over the remainder of the season.

7.4 WEED CONTROL

The protection of the crop against competition from weed plants is an important factor in the reduction of limitations to crop growth. It is necessary to control weeds to the point of their elimination as their presence not only causes competition for water and nutrients from the soil but also they compete for light; indeed many annual weeds develop so quickly in the early season that they can quickly smother a crop to the point of extinction, or induce the development of crooked stems. As a result of their smothering effect they reduce the vigour of the plant and increase the humidity within the crop, thus providing ideal conditions for the multiplication of many pests and diseases.

It is expected that perennial weeds will have been eliminated during the establishment and preparation of the seedbed area but nevertheless localised infestations will occur and should be dealt with by spot treatment during the annual servicing of the bed.

The application of the 'stale seedbed' technique during the normal annual preparation of the bed will effectively reduce the population of annual weed seeds. However, by the nature of their survival mechanisms, the variety of species to be dealt with, their seasons of emergence and the re-introduction each year of seeds from external sources ensures a situation which requires a regular weed control programme for the entire season. This must therefore be an essential feature of successful husbandry.

A control programme for annual weeds is concerned with the period 45 after sowing until the crop is harvested, the period prior to sowing having been dealt with during seedbed preparation. As with any other crop two phases are concerned, that prior to emergence of the seedlings and that after their emergence.

Spring sown crops will normally germinate quickly and there is virtually no chance for pre-emergence treatment as weed seedlings do not appear sufficiently quickly to be able to effect their control before the appearance of the crop. Autumn sown crops, however, provide a long period from mid autumn to early spring for the emergence of weed seedlings, especially those ephemeral types such as Chickweed, Groundsel and Annual Meadow Grass, but these can be quickly eliminated at regular intervals right up until crop emergence by the use of a suitable contact herbicide. At present there is no recognised, suitable herbicide of a residual (soil acting) type which can be used at a pre-emergence stage, and which does not markedly affect the rate of crop growth in the early seedling phase.

This same criticism is also true of the period immediately after germination, until leaf cover occurs, consequently hand weeding is the only available safe method of control. As this is an expensive operation it cannot be over emphasised too greatly that the massive population reductions in annual weed seeds achieved by the stale seedbed operation in seedbed preparation cannot be under estimated, and its importance as an integral part of the continuous weed control pattern becomes apparent.

Once leaf cover has been reached the number of annual weeds which establish is relatively small, but those individuals which do establish grow massively and require control. What little evidence is available suggests that some deciduous subjects will tolerate the use of soil acting herbicides at low concentration at this stage and that these concentrations are sufficient to control the surviving weeds. However, the range of subjects tested has been very limited and no applications should be attempted without trial observations which range over the whole spectrum of species grown and on seedbeds of the same composition and condition. Advice should also be sought from the local A.D.A.S. Advisor.

Chemical weed control on mineral soil seedbeds has been achieved with lenacil (at 1.0 lb. ai/ac), propachlor (at 3.9 lb. ai/ac), simazine (as 1.0 lb. ai/ac) and has provided weed control until the crop is lifted without apparent residual effects on the subsequent crop.

When dealing with soil acting herbicides on such highly anthropomorphic soils (usually with very high organic matter content) it would be prudent for the propagator to reach his own conclusions only after adequate trial observations.

Control programmes for annual weeds must consist therefore of four stages:—

    (i) stale seedbed
   (ii) pre-emergence contact control
  (iii) hand weeding post emergence and
  (iv) soil acting chemicals at leaf cover

7.5 PEST AND DISEASE CONTROL

The protection of the crop against the incidence of pests and diseases is *sine qua non* in the production of seedlings. The incidence of any external agency of this type will necessarily limit crop growth and prevent any real degree of uniformity in the final crop.

Although it would appear that many woody plant seedlings will tolerate light infestations or infections of certain pathogens, it is obvious that any level of incidence will cause some check to growth and control measures should be adopted.

It is virtually impossible to generalise in terms of pest and disease control, as each pathogen or group of pathogens requires its own type of control. However, there are a number of pests and diseases which have a broad spectrum of attack and these can be controlled by routine action over the whole of the seedbed area. Pests and diseases which are specific to a particular crop must be dealt with on an individual basis.

The routine control of pests and diseases falls into two categories, those organisms occurring in the soil and those affecting the leaves and growing tips.

Soil problems would to a certain extent be contained if seedbed sterilisation is practised, however, such agents as slugs and the ubiquitous, if somewhat uncertain, occurrence of the various damping off diseases and Grey Mould *(Botrytis cinerea)* require a continuing preventive programme of chemical control if troublesome outbreaks are to be avoided.

The control of the pests and diseases of the aerial parts of the crop also requires an actively determined policy to protect the crop against such subjects as aphids or adelgids, red spider and the powdery and downy mildews. All these being capable of building up rapidly to large populations, over a wide range of hosts, if climatic conditions are suitable and dramatically checking plant growth in a relatively short time.

These problems, all of general occurrence, will normally be controlled by spraying the whole seedbed area, although the tolerances of particular crops to specific chemicals must first be determined. However, the possibilities of cultural containment by reference to such aspects as the season of sowing, the accurate determination of seedling population and the choice and the siting of shelter belts (as possible alternative hosts) should not be overlooked.

Pests and diseases of particular groups of plants which are likely to prove troublesome require their own specific control programmes. The likely problems and their occurrence can only be determined by reference to the relevant textbooks and by local experience.

The management aspects of pest and disease control tend to be problematical as both the chemicals and the labour involved in application are expensive and some indication of the probability of attack will be needed before control measures are undertaken. The incidence of most attacks is often capricious and it is this uncertainty which often causes a delay in spraying, usually on the grounds of cost, until it is too late. The determination of which system of control will be practised for any particular pest or disease will depend on the likelihood of the incidence of such an attack.

Thus the control of pests and diseases will follow the ensuing pattern:—

(i) routine measures for those pathogens which are non-specific and are ubiquitous in their occurrence, or for those particular pathogens which are regularly annual in their occurrence, or

(ii) specific action if climatic or other signs or conditions indicate the possibility of a particular attack e.g. Mills periods, or

(iii) in the case of unusual outbreaks of infestations, or infections, control measures will only be instituted once an attack has been observed.

Often the effects of certain general control measures are overlooked as their use has become virtually everyday. Captan, for example, which is widely used as a seed dressing has been shown to reduce the germination of certain species of *Picea* and *Pinus,* while BHC has proved toxic to root growth in many gymnosperms as well.

As the particular area of a subject is increased in terms of both seed bed area and/or seedling density, then the likelihood of the incidence of a specific pest or disease is an increasing problem.

Modern pest and disease control depends to a large extent on the use of a wide range of chemicals. The continued and widespread use of such materials however means the necessity for developing a spray programme which is effective in its control, as the repeated use of a limited range of materials will cause the development of biological resistance within a population of a particular pathogen. A programme of control will depend for its success on the varied use of chemicals in succession and/or the single application of a highly effective material, with the latter types the toxicity to the pathogen is often matched by its toxicity to the operator, as well as the possibility of limited tolerance of the crop plant.

Thus the choice of a particular material for use over a wide and varied range of seedling crops will depend on:—

(i) The effectiveness of the chemical in controlling the pathogen(s); nowadays with the complexity of available materials it is wise to seek advice from one's local A.D.A.S. officer who will have access to up-to-date information on the most suitable material (reference to a leaflet such as Entomology Advisory Leaflet *42* of the East Midland Region of A.D.A.S. gives an insight into the diversity of aphidicides alone).

(ii) The susceptibility of the crop plant to a particular chemical must also be monitored carefully, as any check to growth will necessarily affect the ultimate crop quality. Susceptibility may be dependent on concentration and, it is therefore necessary to ensure the correct calibration of one's sprayer and its proper use. As the crop may well be of considerable value the use of alternative, more tolerable, materials should be explored even if they are costly. Attention should also be given to weather conditions which may well induce 'scorch' or other damage under certain circumstances.

(iii) The safety of the operator, as many modern chemicals have high mammalian toxicity, particular attention should be paid to the safety and efficiency of the sprayer, the use of adequate and suitable protective clothing and devices, the adoption of a safe code of practice and the efficient disposal of empty containers.

7.6 SEEDBED MANAGEMENT

From the accumulated comments on seedbed preparation and seedling husbandry it will become apparent that the successful propagation of a crop of seedlings depends very considerably on the implementation and integration of all these facets of production without interruption. In theory this would entail the complete overhaul and preparation of an entire annual seedbed area in each year so that each crop had the best start, this would require two seedbed areas for alternate year production; however, availability of land and capital are unlikely to permit this luxury and a compromise situation must be determined so that an acceptable proportion of the area can be taken out of immediate production and prepared in order to bring it back to a standard condition. This situation however, is not only dictated by the continuous need for seedbed amelioration but is also necessitated by the almost continuous season of seed sowing, which requires the availability of seedbed from midsummer onwards, as summer and autumn sown subjects will be ready well before the season of leaf fall and lifting of the already established crop.

From a general production point of view it is therefore prudent to have at least one third of the total seedbed area not in production during at least the late spring and early summer; so that the various operations and routine maintenance can be carried out.

Seedbed improvement and maintenance, as has already been described is a fairly lengthy operation involving cultivation, incorporating suitable organic matter and grit to improve structure, the topping up of nutrient bases, the correction of pH status, sterilisation if required to control soil borne pests and diseases, and the opportunity for stale seed bedding to minimise annual weed seed populations. All these operations are time consuming and require some expertise which makes the whole process expensive. Thus only a minimum area will be released each year. In effect if a third of the area is prepared each year and 'autumn' sown then the remaining area will have been sown during the previous season, half will have been autumn sown before leaf fall and half spring sown. In practice the area which had been autumn sown the previous season and has been in use for one growing season will be quickly prepared after lifting and used for immediate winter sowing and the later spring sown subjects. The area which has already carried two successive crops is then fallowed and prepared as indicated above to provide the best sequence.

This adherence to the apparent necessity for dividing the cropping area into thirds is not quite as rigid as it might appear as there will be many seeds — especially those which have been stratified or cold stored — which can be sown at either season, depending on the availability of seedbed at each season, and the cropping programme envisaged, so that ample opportunity for changes in cropping policy and a general flexibility can be maintained.

ASSOCIATED READING

'The Farmer's Weather', M.A.F.F. Bull *165* H.M.S.O. (1964)
Scientific Horticulture, Vol *17*, H.E.A. (1964-5).
'Irrigation', M.A.F.F. Bull *138*, H.M.S.O. (1974).
'Water for Irrigation', M.A.F.F. Bull. *202,* H.M.S.O. (1967).

HARDY WOODY
PLANTS FROM SEED

'Irrigation Guide', M.A.F.F., S.T.L.71 (1975).

'Spring Frosts' For. Comm. Bull. *18*, H.M.S.O. (1946)

'Frost protection of fruit crops by water sprinkling', M.A.F.F., S.T.L. *125* (1971).

'Weed Control in Nursery Stock Production', M.A.F.F., S.T.L. *69* (1970).

'Redshank, Pale Persicaria, Knotgrass and Black Bindweed,' M.A.F.F., A.L. *432* (1975).

'Common Chickweed', M.A.F.F., A.L. *528* (1973).

'Perennial Bindweeds', M.A.F.F., A.L. *450* (1973).

'Couch', M.A.F.F., A.L. *89* (1974).

'Weed Control — Thistles', M.A.F.F., A.L. *51* (1973).

'Bracken and its control', M.A.F.F., A.L. *190* (1974).

'Weed Control — Rushes'. M.A.F.F., A.L. *433*(1973).

'Pathology of Trees and Shurbs', T.R. Peace, O.U.P., (1962).

'Pests of Ornamental Plants', M.A.F.F., Bull. *97,* H.M.S.O. (1974).

'Conifer Woolly Aphids *(Adelgidae)* in Britain', For. Comm. *42,* H.M.S.O. (1971).

'Rusts of British Forest Trees', For. Comm. Bklt. *4,* (1955).

'Grey Mould in Forest Nurseries', For. Comm. Lflt. *50*(1969).

'Red Spider Mite on Outdoor Crops', M.A.F.F., A.L. *226* (1973).

'Web-forming Caterpillars', M.A.F.F., A.L. *40* (1974).

'Slugs and Snails', M.A.F.F., A.L. *115,* (1974).

'Cutworms', M.A.F.F., A.L. *225* (1972).

'Crown Gall and Leafy Gall', M.A.F.F., A.L. *253* (1974).

'Survey of Losses of First Year Conifer Seeds and Seedlings in Forestry Commission Nurseries 1972' For. Comm. R. and S. Paper *103* (1973).

'The Potato Cyst Eelworm (Great Britain) Order 1973', M.A.F.F., S.I. *1059*, (1975).

'Horticultural Sprayers for small areas', M.A.F.F. S.T.L. *131* (1971).

'Agricultural Chemicals Approval Scheme', M.A.F.F. (Revised annually).

'Murphy Nurseryman's Book' Murphy Chemical Ltd., Wheathampstead, St. Albans, Herts.

Appendix 1
Commercial Sources of Tree & Shrub Seeds

A. EUROPEAN SEEDHOUSES

Mosbacher Gehölz-und Waldsamen,
Gammelsbach,
Postfach 1123,
D-6124 Bearfelden,
West Germany.

Renz Nachf. GmbH & Co. KG.,
727 Nagold — Emmingen,
West Germany.

Paul Raeymaekers,
Turnhoutsebaan 143,
Mol B-2400,
Belgium.

Establissements Versepuy,
Le Puy — 43000,
Haute Loire,
France.

Vilmorin-Andrieux,
Service Graine d'Arbres,
La Menitre,
49250 Beaufort-en-Vallee,
Maine et Loire,
France.

Søren Levinsen,
Kollerød Bygade 25,
3450 — Allerød,
Denmark.

A. J. Frost,
7080 Börkop,
Denmark.

H. Den Ouden & Zoon B.V.,
The Old Farm Nurseries,
Boskoop,
Holland.

B.V. 'Bommwekerij Udenhout',
Schoorstraat 21,
Postbus 31,
Udenhout,
Holland.

Van Dijk & Co. B.V.,
Enhuizen,
Holland.

Barilli and Biagi,
1-40. 100 Bologna,
Casella Postale 1645-AD,
Italy.

Florsilva Ansaloni,
1-40. 100 Bologna,
Casella Postale 2100-EL,
Italy.

Franz Kluger,
A-1020, Vienna 2,
Obere Augartenstrasse 18,
Austria.

Seed Branch,
Forestry Commission Research Station,
Alice Holt Lodge,
Wrecclesham,
Farnham,
Surrey,
England.

B. NORTH AMERICAN SEEDHOUSES

F. W. Schumacher & Co.,
Sandwich,
Mass. 02563,
U.S.A.

Silvaseed Company,
P.O. Box 118,
Roy,
Washington 98580,
U.S.A.

Vans Pines Inc.,
West Olive,
Michigan 49460,
U.S.A.

V.B.M. Seeds,
4607 Wendover Blvd.,
Alexandria,
Louisiana 71301,
U.S.A.

Lawyers Nursery,
Plains,
Montana 59859,
U.S.A.

Northplan Seed Producers,
P.O. Box 9107,
Moscow,
Idaho, 83843,
U.S.A.

C. OTHERS

Nindethana Seed Service,
Narrikup,
Western Australia 6326,
Australia.

H. G. Kershaw,
P.O. Box 88,
Mona Vale,
N.S.W. 2103,
Australia.

Chandra,
Upper Cart Road,
P.O. Kalimpong 734301,
India.

P. Kohli and Son,
Park Road,
Srinagar,
Kashmir,
India.

Appendix 2

Mycorrhizal Associations

It has been recognised for a considerable period of time that many tree and shrub seeds, and especially seeds of coniferous subjects, only succeed in establishing themselves satisfactorily as seedlings, when germinated in a seedbed sited on, or containing, soil in which the particular species has previously been growing. Under natural conditions many plants exhibiting this tendency only produce a poorly developed and specialised root system which is then amplified to normal proportions by the development of a mycorrhizal association. In simple terms a mycorrhizal association is derived from a mutually beneficial arrangement between a plant and a fungus or variety of fungi. The arrangement involves the exchange of materials useful to each partner, in this particular instance the fungus replaces the feeding root system of the plant and extracts water and nutrients from the soil which are 'passed on' to the plant, in return the fungus appears to obtain elaborated carbohydrate materials from the host plant. The various types of inter-relationship and levels of dependence between plant and fungus are complex and at present still imperfectly understood; further references are therefore provided for the interested reader.

If a plant which normally grows in its natural environment with such an association is germinated in the absence of suitable fungi, it is reasonable to suppose that its subsequent development and rate of growth may well be considerably hindered and it may possibly be sufficiently dependent on such an association to be incapable of developing a normal root system.

The presence of these root/fungus associations or mycorrhiza in higher plants is extremely widespread and the greater proportion of woody plants develop this type of association in some degree. The degree of dependence, however, varies from species to species — some being capable of normal root development in the absence of a suitable association or in unsuitable soils while others are very nearly totally dependent and will not thrive unless suitable fungi are present and soil conditions are right for the development of a mycorrhiza.

In the large scale production of tree and shrub seedlings it is quite possible to innoculate the soil of the seedbed with suitable soil or leaf mould to ensure the presence and availability of the necessary variety and quantity of mycorrhizal fungi. The effect will be most beneficial if there is sufficient fungal presence in the seedbed such that the emerging radicle of the seedling would quickly come into contact with suitable fungi for the rapid   53 development of a mycorrhiza. Biologists concerned in the study of mycorrhiza are still relatively unsure of the necessity for or the abilities of these associations because of the difficulties attached to their culture away from the soil, in consequence there is divergence of opinion in terms of practicalities in relation to applied knowledge. Even among propagators the value of 'innoculation' of the soil is viewed by some with scepticism. However, the practical evidence amassed from observations and trials indicates the value of a seedbed made up with a proportion leaf litter, (or substituted organic matter in part) in promoting the improvement of seedling quality. But it is quite feasible that this value is a function of the improved general environment of the root development medium, i.e. aeration, nitrate availability, etc. provided by these materials, although all these factors would also benefit mycorrhizas and produce their associated advantages. It is certainly evident from the currently available literature that it is just as important to provide desirable environmental conditions for fungal development as to have the fungi present. The only factor which appears to depress the intensity of mycorrhizal formation is excessive nitrogen fertilisation, as may occur through a feeding programme. This developed overdependence on immediately available nitrogen may well be detrimental to the ultimate establishment of the seedling on transplanting, because it engenders an ill-developed mycorrhizal system.

Evidence also suggests that mycorrhizal formation is enhanced by the presence of large quantities of organic matter, especially if it maintains a pH in the range of 4.0 to 6.0.

However, the necessity for innoculation may not be vital as long as adequate organic matter is present to encourage quick fungal development; the actual innoculation being produced by fungal 'spore rain' which is continually occurring from the atmosphere. This would then mitigate the arguments against seedbed sterilisation, however it may be important for sterilisation to be carried out sufficiently in advance of sowing that such fungal populations have had an opportunity to re-establish themselves before germination occurs. The only drawbacks to this system would be the elimination of those potential mycorrhiza formers which do not spore or which spore for a very limited season.

A.2.1. DUNEMANN SEEDBEDS

The use of leaf litter as a means of innoculating a seedbed with suitable fungi for mycorrhizal associations leads on to its consideration as a germinating medium for seeds in the forest, woodland or thicket floor; the natural seedbed will be leaf litter and similar detritus. This idea may be stretched a stage further and in addition to providing the required fungal associations, further aspects of the natural environment may be simulated to increase the successful establishment and development of seedlings. Those conditions suitable for forest tree subjects could be provided by a reasonably deep layer of decomposing leaf mould overlying a layer of sharp drainage material. At and after germination the entire seedbed would be shaded to reproduce the effect of the forest canopy.

Such a developed system was devised by Alfred Dunemann who patented a technique in the mid 1930's in Germany. The system was introduced to this country in the early 1950's and has found limited use for the production of coniferous subjects on forest tree nurseries. The use and value of these areas was well documented by Aldhous (1962).

A.2.11 CONSTRUCTION OF DUNEMANN SEEDBEDS

The specification provides for the erection of the seedbeds on a suitable pattern using sideboards to a height of fourteen inches (35cm) and five to six feet apart (1½-2m). The basal four to six inches (10-15cm) is filled with small weathered clinker which is levelled off with small grade ash. This provides the drainage layer. The frame is now filled with leaf litter from the forest floor which is well firmed as it is added, this is finally levelled off at some two inches (5cm) from the top of the boards. This is topped off with sifted leaf mould. Dunemann specified particularly that the leaf litter should be a mixture of that provided by the Norway Spruce *(Picea abies)* and the Sitka Spruce *(Picea sitchensis)* and that the final sifting should be Beech *(Fagus sylvatica)*.

This system, pursued rigidly, has proved an expensive item to produce and as might be expected has been modified in practice. Experience has shown that alterations can be made to the system without any detriment to crop production. Trials conducted over a wide variety of seedlings have shown that specific leaf moulds are not particularly advantageous and that virtually any coniferous leaf litter will suffice. Observation also indicates that as long as a significant proportion (about half) of the litter is coniferous, extending it with other material such as hardwood leaf litter, peat or spent hops is not detrimental and may be a necessity if suitable coniferous material is not readily available. This then supposes that the major factor provided by the organic matter is purely physical condition. Current information suggests that very many fungi will form mycorrhizal associations with one species of hosts while one host will associate with many fungi on the same plant at the same time, hence as long as some innoculum is provided the specificity of the source may not necessarily be significant.

The provision of sharp drainage has not proved an essential factor so long as the underlying soil has been well cultivated and is adequately drained. The depth of leaf litter has not proved critical and need not exceed six to eight inches (15-20cm) for fibrous rooted subjects such as most conifers.

A.2.12. SEEDLING PRODUCTION

Dunemann's specification provided for broadcast sowing and then covering the seed with sifted leaf mould. Prior to sowing, the bed should have been well watered and thereafter kept fairly damp. Shading for the seedlings was provided by a 60% cover of wooden laths or conifer branches.

The seed on such a seedbed can be sown at up to twice the density normally recommended for a mineral soil seedbed, although germination rates have not proved to be appreciably higher, the survival of the seedlings is very much greater and productivity from the seedbed is twice that expected 55 from a mineral soil seedbed, even with the greater density which would usually anticipate some losses.

As a feature this type of seedbed is a relatively expensive investment and as such it is important that productivity is maintained. It should be ensured that all seeds requiring treatments to overcome dormancy have received them prior to sowing, as failure to germinate in the first spring would prove costly, and that viability and sowing rates have accurately been assessed.

Covering the seeds with sifted leaf mould is less desirable than covering with grit as the latter material doesn't matt when watered and doesn't lift in wads when germination occurs. Grit also eases any rewetting of the seedbed should it dry out and allows the easy removal of weed seedlings without undue disturbances.

'Damping off' diseases would appear to be very much less significant on Dunemann beds but the reasons for this are not obvious. The chief pests of such seedbeds are mice and voles, and foxes who find the texture of the seedbed ideal for burying contraband chicken or game-bird carcases during hard weather.

Weeds are rarely a problem although woodland tree seeds introduced with leaf litter can germinate in considerable quantities and create a problem, the chief culprits being Holly, Yew and Birch.

Published results have indicated that one year old seedlings from a Dunemann seedbed are 30% taller than seedlings from mineral soil seedbeds, although the root systems of each sample were strictly comparable. This may not be unexpected for although the improved growing conditions may allow greater stem development, the increased density would preclude a greater increase in each individual root system. The increase in height may also be related to the continued growth of the seedling later in the autumn, giving a longer growing season, this also enhances the development of the greater proportion of matured wood and a greater degree of bud development and maturity. This improves winter survival/storage and gives the seedling a better start in the following spring.

A.2.13 CONCLUSIONS

The costs of establishment of such a seedbed are high in comparison with a mineral soil seedbed although its maintenance is no greater as it has a (relatively) long life. The most significant additional cost is provided by the necessity for an adequate irrigation system as it is imperative that a seedbed comprising solely of organic materials should not be allowed to dry out, as rewetting is a major problem.

Although this system may have doubtful economic advantage in forestry practice, it has proved a very useful method for the production of valuable ornamental coniferous subjects and the technique may well have a place in nursery practice especially for those subjects in which the seed itself is a major item of cost. The benefits of increased size and vigour of the seedlings is also an additional bonus when speed in the production of the saleable crop is a critical factor.

ASSOCIATED READING

Aldhous,J.R. (1962), 'A Survey of Dunemann Seedbeds in Great Britain'; Quart. For.*56*(3): 185.

Grant,W. (1952), 'The Dunemann System of Nursery Practice'; Quart, J. For. *46*: 247.

Handley, W.R.C. (1963) 'Mycorrhizal Associations and Calluna Heathland Afforestation', For. Comm. Bull. *36* H.M.S.O.

Harley,J.L: (1956) 'The Mycorrhiza of Forest Trees', Endeavour *25* (1); 43.

Harley, J.L. (1969), 'The Biology of Mycorrhiza', Leonard Hill, London, 2nd. ed.

Hutt,P.A. (1956) 'The Dunemann Nursery System', Quart, J. For.,*50*, 155 and 332.

Mikola P., (1973), 'Mycorrhizal Symbiosis in Forestry Practice', in 'Ectomycorrhizae, their ecology and physiology', ed. G.C. Marks and T.T. Kozlowski, Academic Press, p. 383 et seq.

Raynor, M.C. (1945) 'Trees and Toadstools', Faber and Faber, London.

Appendix 3

Seed Treatments

A.3.1 ACID DIGESTION OF HARD SEEDCOATS

Seedcoat dormancy of these types is due to the development of protective materials which surround the seed. It is not important whether the actual tissue is a condition of the seedcoat proper or of a fruit layer, the practical effect is still the same. These protective layers either cause impermeability to water or less often impermeability to gases, both of which prevent germination; occasionally the seedcoat simply acts by restricting embryo expansion.

Most usually this type of seed dormancy is caused by the uniform development of hard often fairly brittle substances, as occurs in many Leguminous subjects and related types. Less often the thickened seedcoat has a more fibrous structure as in *Rosa, Crataegus* etc.

Exceptionally the fruit structure may develop a tough pliant, as opposed to hard, condition and this is particularly difficult to overcome.

In a few, but nevertheless important, subjects these two types of dormancy controls are combined causing real practical problems.

Although there are a number of ways of overcoming this problem, so that germination can be induced as required, the use of concentrated acids is still one of the most reliable and accurate methods.

The reduction of hard seedcoats by digestion with concentrated acid is nevertheless a technique requiring some considerable expertise in the handling of the materials, as the process is hazardous both for the operator and for the survival of the seed.

Concentrated acids are dangerous materials to handle and care should be exercised at all times. Unless specialised equipment is available: glass, earthenware or wooden receptacles should be used for holding the acid and for the digestion process; metal containers may well disintegrate or come apart at the joins, as the welds become eaten away by the reaction with the acid; and plastic containers should also be avoided as this type of material may degenerate quickly with the rapid rise in temperature which can occur if the reaction goes awry.

Plastic utensils should only be used if moulded in one piece and are of thick gauge and will resist high temperatures.

The seed is treated by immersing the cleaned and extracted sample in twice its volume of concentrated acid. Commercial 'oleum' is normally used, i.e. commercial 95% sulphuric acid (SG:1.84), although certain specific subjects are treated with nitric acid. The seed is left to digest for a predetermined period so that the seedcoat is reduced to a level at which the seed will imbibe.

It is also relevant to conduct the digestion at a standard temperature as the actual length of treatment (i.e. the rate of reaction) required will be a function of temperature. In practice a temperature of 18-20°C is most reasonable to maintain and control.

In Order to ensure an even and uniform digestion the mixture of seeds and acid is *gently* and *regularly* stirred so that any localised increase in reaction, with its consequent build up in temperature, will be prevented. Rapid stirring should be avoided as the increased aeration is likely to add a new dimension to the reaction and a rapid build up of temperature occurs with associated damage to the embryo.

As soon as the correct end state is reached the seeds should be quickly removed from the acid or the acid decanted off from the seed and the sample plunged into a large volume of cold water containing a very small quantity of washing soda. This causes the digestive action to be arrested. The sample is then rinsed and drained. The seed may then be sown directly or dried and stored for a short period.

It is relevant to start with seeds at air temperature, if seeds are removed from cold storage they will almost certainly develop a moisture film from atmospheric condensation. This moisture will then react with the acid causing an unnecessary build up of temperature.

Information on the length of time that is required for the treatment of some subjects is available from various sources, but it is always advisable to start from scratch and assess each sample individually as the degree of development of a hard seedcoat, and hence the period of digestion, varies extensively from source to source and year to year for the same subject. It is advisable to avoid treatment of too large a 'lot' of seed (over 10 kg) as overheating may occur and this may not be easily controlled in a large mass, and and uneven effect may be produced.

In those seeds in which digestion causes a charring of the seed covering, regular stirring abrades this effect and allows continued digestion of the inner layers. The development of a charred layer causes a partial impediment to continued digestion and in consequence the time lapse required for full digestion is no longer adequately monitored and reliable treatments cannot be expected.

The period of digestion is determined by a pilot investigation which is conducted several days in advance on a small quantity of seed. The seed is immersed in the acid and a sample is extracted and washed at regular intervals so that the degree of digestion can be monitored. Assessment of seedcoat reduction is made by soaking the digested seeds for 24 hours in water and determining the number of imbibed seeds at the end of this period. When reduction to a suitable level, i.e. when virtually all the seeds imbibe, has been achieved the time lapse is noted and used for the main sample. The test requires continual observation if the final stage is to be determined ac-

59

curately; with many seeds the degree of digestion to a level at which imbibition will occur is not critical to the survival of the seed, and further digestion can occur for some time without undue detriment, indeed, it may proceed until such time as the seed itself is exposed.

This initial investigation should be conducted with the *same proportions of seed and acid* to be used for the main process as the efficiency of digestion by the acid will decline as the reaction continues and the acid becomes 'spent' so that the process is continually slowing. This situation (the variation in proportion of acid to seed) also accounts, in all probability, for many of the references to widely varying times required for the digestion of the same seeds.

This ratio of volumes suggested is merely a useful rule of thumb as the actual amount of acid required will vary with the quantity of material needing to be digested. Thus as a constant ratio is used samples with thicker/tougher coats will require more digestion and as the acid becomes 'spent' will take proportionally longer, also accounting for variations in treatment time.

Although many seeds have sucessfully been treated by using this technique, most subjects which have been traditionally subjected to the treatment have only required it because late collection and dry storage have enhanced the development of such an intractable seedcoat that it has been the only way to overcome this inhibition to germination in the short term. Thus the collection of seed prior to full ripeness, and moist storage or immediate sowing will obviate the necessity for such a treatment.

The hard seedcoats of typical leguminous subjects do not normally require any special seed treatment prior to acid digestion as they are uniformly dry and impermeable: however those subjects, mostly members of the Rosaceae, which have a more reticulate structure require drying prior to digestion as fresh achenes usually contain water. This water held in the tissue permits the passage of acid into the seed and subsequently damage to the seed tissues.

Most experience of acid digestion of seedcoats has been based on the treatment of seeds of leguminous subjects and a number of other large seeds which reduce readily. With these subjects the assessment of the end stage can be determined fairly readily. However, the treatment of the seeds of rosaceous subjects is not nearly so clear cut and is not easy to assess the end stage; in practice seeds of this type (*Rosa and Contoneaster*) are digested to remove the greater proportion of the hard material and are finished off by a period of warm stratification so that damage to the actual seed is avoided— the recommendations for the treatment of *Rosa laxa* seed.

A third group of seeds, which *Hamamelis* is a typical example, do not respond to a simple treatment with sulphuric acid because the outer seedcoat or pericarp is 'tough' rather than 'hard' and this acid does not digest such material satisfactorily; in these instances the tough coat should be reduced with nitric acid and subsequently the inner hard coat is digested with sulphuric acid.

Examples of those subjects which have successfully responded to treatment by acid digestion of the seedcoat include:

a) *Seeds responding to a simple sulphuric acid digestion:-*

Cercis siliquastrum
Gleditsia triacanthos
Gymnocladus dioicus
Koelreuteria paniculata
Cornus mas

b) *Seeds requiring nitric and sulphuric acid digestion:-*
Daphne mezereum
Hamamelis spp.
Tilia spp.

c) *Seeds requiring sulphuric acid digestion followed by a*
short period of warm stratification:-
Cotoneaster spp.
Rosa spp.

It is important to emphasise that the *use of concentrated acids is hazardous* and that *care should be exercised in handling* such *materials*. In particular it should be remembered *never add water to acid* as the reaction will be violent and dangerous.

A.3.21. CONTROLLED STRATIFICATION WITH A CONTROLLED ENVIRONMENT

Available literature merely indicates that many seeds require dormancy breaking conditions which are satisfied by a particular period of chilling, and that this is conventionally carried out by the process of stratification. It is apparent however, that when the propagator comes to carry out this exercise there are many details to be considered of a practical nature which are not fully described.

Stratification normally refers to the exposure of a dormant seed sample to a period of chilling (it may also however, refer to exposure to a period of warmth in order to aid seedcoat decomposition or immature embryo development).

Chilling may be defined as the exposure of the fully imbibed dormant seed to a period of cold temperature: however, 'cold' temperature is a relative term and can only be related to the particular climatic conditions under which a species has evolved (and indeed in those plants with an extensive geographical range this factor may vary with provenance). Subjects from the warmer regions of the temperate climate may be stimulated by temperatures below 10°C, whereas plants from the colder temperate regimes may respond only to temperatures below 5°C or even 3°C. Those subjects from the limits of cold temperate regions and sub-arctic conditions often respond eccentrically, especially if much of the winter in their normal habitat is below freezing point: it would appear that sub-zero temperatures are not active in the stimulation affected by chilling; and that these plants have relatively short chilling requirements, often at relatively high temperatures (a pattern which corresponds with the spring thaw). Thus a reasonably detailed knowledge of the native habitat of a particular species is a basic essential if some guide to the chilling requirements of the sample is to be assessed.

The action of chilling is not precisely clear, it would appear that germination is prevented by a chemical which inhibits embryo development, and   61 that chilling neutralises its effect by stimulating the production of a promoter chemical, which in turn eventually reaches a sufficient concentration to overcome the effect of the inhibitor. The problem is knowing the mechanism which triggers this reaction and what role the quantitative effect of cold fulfils. This pattern is probably true for broadleaf trees although in conifers the responses appear to be less certain.

It is important with small batches of high value seed that dormancy is completely broken (insofar as this can be achieved): so that all potentially germinable seeds can be induced to develop: thus artificial treatment to achieve adequate chilling together with a minimisation of any losses is paramount for economic production. Seed may be stratified by exposure to normal winter conditions but this may be unsatisfactory, practically, for those subjects having a chilling requirement in excess of that provided under usual climatic conditions. Accuracy in this provision can therefore only be effectively achieved under controlled conditions. The provision of a cold store or refrigerator capable of temperature adjustments at the 0 to 5°C level is necessary. Although this may be significant for all seed it is not always practicable with large quantities of the lower value subjects; and economic considerations may dictate that a proportion of losses is acceptable with less critical conditions.

In practice the chilling effect is achieved by mixing the fully imbibed seed with a medium, which will hold sufficient moisture to maintain the water status of the seed while it is being exposed to its period of cold; and for this purpose various materials have been used—peat, sand, peat and sand mixtures, vermiculite etc. Whatever material is selected it is important that its moisture content is only sufficiently adequate to maintain the water status of the already imbibed seed: so that waterlogging is prevented and good aeration is maintained. This last factor is often disregarded but effective chilling induces a considerable amount of respiratory activity within the seed and the necessity for adequate oxygen becomes significant. Thus it will be important to determine a particular level for the moisture content of the medium used and subsequently the ratio of seed to medium employed. By limiting these variables a standard technique can be employed which produces the correct environment and reproducible results. The real practical problems are concerned with ensuring maximum survival within the seed sample during chilling, and this is largely a function of developing a stratifying medium which prevents waterlogging and maintains aeration. The selection of a stratifying medium may be affected by various considerations and these might include ease of distribution at sowing, the ease with which the seed may be separated from the medium should this be necessary, the uniformity of its water holding and its resistance to compaction. Thus bags or jars containing a mixture of seed and medium should be turned and shaken regularly to prevent compaction and waterlogging at the bottom and to ensure even temperature gradients.

It is not feasible to make recommendations for a stratifying medium, as materials and conditions vary so much from nursery to nursery: however a brief description of one successful method may be of value. Irish Sphagnum Peat in a dry condition was put through a sieve to produce a uniform consistency, 4 volumes of this peat as sieved (i.e. not compacted) was wetted with 1 volume of water so that when a handful of the soaked peat was squeezed tightly it just produced a drop of water. Four volumes of this damp peat was

then mixed evenly with 1 volume of seed and the whole then placed in a polythene bag *with a label;* tied and labelled on the outside.

An assessment of the period required for chilling is difficult to determine accurately because of seasonal variations, varying patterns of reaction
within samples and variations between sources, but general trends can be observed and will provide a guide. Accurate determination of the chilling requirements for each sample is necessary, as experience suggests that under
nursery conditions the viability of a sample begins to decline after the
optimum chilling period has been reached. This accuracy depends for its
successful assessment on the removal of any other constraints to germination
especially chemical conditions within the seedcoat; and on the complete imbibition of the sample prior to the commencement of chilling, so that the
chilling effect begins immediately and the beginning of the treatment is not
taken up with imbibition, so masking when the chilling actually begins and
producing an unreliable measurement. It also requires a sampling technique
capable of determining the germination capacity at any particular time so
that the optimum period of chilling can be pinpointed.

If cold temperature dormancy conditions can be overcome by controlled
chilling it is important that the optimum chilling period should be accurately
monitored: this requires the development of a satisfactory sampling
technique. Germination of seed at relatively warm temperatures is generally
vigorous if the seeds are removed from chilling and sown without delay,
therefore the sowing should be timed to coincide with the advent of warm
soil temperatures in the spring. Reference to weather records relevant to the
site will provide a suitable proposed date for sowing and the commencement
date for chilling can be calculated back from this date accordingly: this of
course cannot allow for variations from the norm but is the only method
feasible. The available evidence suggests that the normal temperate climate
subjects will show best germination in the field at about 10°C, increasing
temperatures in excess of this often show progressive developments of
secondary dormancy. Thus the batch of seed will commence its chilling on
this calculated date, but a suitably sized sample should be extracted prior to
this date so that chilling can be begun in advance of the main batch. It can
then be sub-sampled in order to assess germination capacity and the
optimum period for treatment.

SAMPLING PROCEDURE

1) Take a sufficiently large sample of seed — say 25 seeds for each proposed
   sampling date at a suitable period prior to commencement of treatment
   of main batch — possibly 3 to 4 weeks.
2) Mix seeds uniformly with stratifying medium using standard procedure
   (i.e. moisture content and seed/medium ratio).
3) Store seed at room temperature for four to seven days until seed is fully
   imbibed.
4) Store at required temperature — the chilling treatment.
5) Sample at weekly intervals, three weeks either side of the normally
   expected optimum period being sure to select the sample randomly.
6) Check germination by sowing a sample of (25) seeds in a seed tray and
   germinate in a warm glasshouse (about 12°C), this may require up to
   three weeks to produce a result: as an alternative and quicker method   63

(25) seeds are placed on a damp filter paper: this is then incubated at 20°C, the radicles emerge after 48 hours or so and potential germination can be assessed.

This sampling system produces an accurate measurement of the chilling period, and the main batch can be removed from chilling and sown at the correct period for the stimulation of best germination.

With those subjects in which germination, or at least radicle emergence, is observable within a short period of time — say 48 hours or thereabouts then it would be possible to direct sample the entire batch and so avoid pilot sampling.

In those subjects in which chitting (or radicle emergence) will occur at low temperatures, it is possible that chitting of some seeds will occur if there is significant variation of chilling requirement within the batch, so that chitting of the seeds with the shortest chilling will occur before those seeds needing the longest chill have been satisfied. If radicle emergence develops beyond the overall length of the seed then damage and losses may well occur at sowing: it is therefore important to decide on a compromise date of sowing so that the greatest proportion of viable seeds can be successfully germinated. Thus a balance between early chitting and insufficient chill is achieved, this problem is particularly prevalent in many rosaceous subjects, especially *Sorbus* and *Crataegus*.

Once a pattern for a particular species has been observed it is also possible to assess when the chilling treatment should begin so that maximum field emergence can be achieved; this can be calculated from an average of chilling periods and the date at which seedbed temperature will be sufficiently warm for a quick germination to occur, (10-12°C). However, samples from differing sources, prior storage treatments and yearly harvests often produce significantly variable results.

The graphical representation of results is shown in figure 2 but these should only be regarded as a general picture from which can be derived a number of pointers:-

(i) the relatively short period over which a maximum emergence will be induced, and so the significance of determining this chilling period accurately,

(ii) the varying requirements even of species from the same genus,

(iii) the maximum percentage emerging is from the basic sample of seeds and will, of course, vary with the viability; in the particular examples, viability was 80% (i.e. the maximum possible energence was 80%).

ASSOCIATED READING

Barton, L.V. (1956), 'Gathering, stratification and sowing of seed', Proc. Plant Prop; Soc. *6:* 96.

Blundell,J.B. (1973), 'Rootstock seed growth improved', Gard. Chron. *174*(1) : 16.

Blundell, J.B. & G.A.D. Jackson (1971) 'Rose seed germination in relation to stock production', Rose Ann. 1970, Lond.: 129.

Sladen,N.A. (1973) 'The effect of the moisture medium ratio and the duration of stratification on the rate of germination of 'Antonovka' apple seed', Plant Prop. *19* (1) : 12.

Appendix 4

The Practical Assessment of Viability

Any technique which determines the viability of a seed sample is only of practical value if it also gives some useful indication of the ability to produce plants in the seedbed. Thus an assessment of whether a seed is merely alive is not really sufficient, it is also necessary to be able to determine how vigorous the embryo is in terms of developing into an established seedling.

When a seed sample, naturally, exhibits no dormancy conditions and is fully after-ripened, *i.e.* it is capable of germination when subjected to suitable environmental conditions, then an ordinary germination test will give a measure of seed viability. Such a system can also be applied to seeds which develop dormancy controls of the hard or impermeable seedcoat type after they have been subjected to a treatment which has reduced this limitation, the test can also be used to give an indication of the vigour of the sample as far as seedbed establishment is concerned.

If an individual seed is large enough then a simple cutting test will allow visual observation of the embryo, and with experience an assessment can be made of the viability: it is not easy, however, to determine failing viability when a seed has recently been dried, albeit only marginally but sufficiently that tissues have been damaged. Visual observation does allow dead and necrotic areas to be recognised which, with experience, can give a measure of the quality of the sample.

The measurement of the viability of a seed sample in conventional circumstances is achieved in a seed laboratory by causing germination and then assessing the resultant seedlings in terms of their ability to establish successfully as plants. Even with ideal conditions however the time involved in completing the exercise may be lengthy, and indeed, this period will be extensively prolonged if it is necessary to overcome cold temperature dormancy conditions before germination can be initiated. Thus the value of the exercise may be lost for many hardy, woody subjects which exhibit more complex dormancy problems.

If, however, some quick biochemical test could be applied to a sample which would give demonstrably comparable results with the germination test, then the time factor could be eliminated and the information would be available at a useful period for practical sowing purposes.

The Tetrazolium Test provides such a measure. The process depends on a colourless liquid being imbibed by the seed, the active ingredient is then 65 reduced in living tissue to produce an insoluble non-diffusable, red coloured substance which effectively dyes the living tissue pink or red and leaves dead material in the embryo uncoloured. This pattern can then be assessed and with experience can allow a measure of the viability of the seeds and the vigour of the seedlings. Such an elegantly simple system is of additional value because the results can be assessed regardless of any dormancy controls which are still present in the seed.

The reaction depends on a one per cent centaqueous solution of 2.3.5. - triphenyl-tetrazolium chloride (or bromide), and for most effective results the maintenance of reasonably neutral conditions (pH 6-7). The chemical is light sensitive and for the most dependable results the period of the test should be conducted without undue exposure to light.

It is necessary to emphasise that, for most seedling propagators, the conditions of a laboratory are not usually available; however this test can be carried out with a minimum of equipment, and although results may not be of the standard which can be achieved under ideal laboratory conditions, they can be used to give a very reasonable assessment of viability. Although the interpretation of the amount and quality of living tissue under these circumstances is subjective, experience will soon produce accurate indications.

The test is carried out quite simply by cutting each seed in two so that the embryo is sufficiently exposed for observation. The seed or part seed is then immersed in sufficient solution and maintained at a warm temperature (20°C - 30°C) in the dark. The reaction is usually adequately complete for assessment purposes after twelve hours, although it may be preferable in some cases to leave for twenty-four hours.

Large seeds can readily be assessed with a naked eye but smaller seeds will need observation with a hand lens. To ease the various activities, especially with small seeds, it may be a useful investment to obtain a low power binocular microscope so that the initial cutting and the final assessment can be improved.

Appendix 5

Purchasing Seed

In the initial development of a programme for seedling propagation, a decision will be made which determines the numbers of a particular subject which are to be produced. This figure can then be divided by the anticipated yield of the crop, in terms of the number of acceptable grade seedlings which are produced per unit area; and this then determines the amount of seedbed required.This is necessarily a simple calculation, which will operate satisfactorily provided that all the husbandry and climatic factors involved do not produce extreme situations.

One of the most irritating of marginal difficulties however, which besets the propagator of seedlings, is the problem of determining the quantity of seed to obtain, in order to be able to produce this predetermined quantity of crop. Experience operators will of course know these figures but it is the inexperienced who will be seeking information, and a knowledge of the seedcount of a sample is of paramount importance if adequate seed is to be purchased. This determination could be made more exactly if the viability of the sample was also known; in practice however this figure has to be estimated from experience and available information on the basis of source, season and storage practices prior to dispatch. Finally the propagator must introduce his own variable — the field factor — so that the expected loss rate of these potential plants can also be accounted for, in the determination.

A combination of all these factors will also allow an assessment to be made of the relative costs of different types of seeds, for it only requires a cursory glance at a catalogue of tree and shrub seeds to ascertain that prices of closely related subjects can vary considerably. Many factors must influence the price of a seed sample — availability in a particular season, rarity, quality, purity, difficulties of collection and/or extraction, desirability of provenance — but primarily it is normally seedcount; for ultimately the question posed by the commercial producer will be 'How many potential plants are being purchased?' and this in turn will derive very coarsely the contribution to the costs of production which are attributable to the seed itself.

Obviously such figures only give a rough indication and take no account of viability, seasonal fluctuations in seed size and varying provenances; but some yardstick must be accepted, in order to be able to purchase sufficient seed or determine how expensive a particular subject proves to be. The increasing cost of seed also means tighter budgetary controls in this aspect of 67 production so that the propagator will wish to purchase only sufficient seed; because of this latter factor it is important to scan all available sources of seed so that the best purchase price can be obtained — although the cheapest is not necessarily the best: provenance and reliability being more important than cheapness. Business confidence is also an important aspect when dealing with overseas suppliers and this cannot necessarily be measured in financial terms. However, when dealing with even a limited range of suppliers some comparison of prices may well pay dividends, especially if counts and viability measurements can be obtained.

When comparing prices from different sources it is as well to take account of a number of additional contributory costs such as:-

Packing
Certification
Insurance and Duties
Freight

which are incurred, and which will vary according to source and distance of travel, these are most satisfactorily distributed on a weight basis when apportioning the costs per item in a total lot.

AN EXERCISE IN COMPARING SEED SOURCE ON A COST BASIS

The figures are extracted from the 1975 catalogues of six European seed-houses. The errors of comparison are necessarily compounded by fluctuating exchange rates. The figures do, however, indicate the necessity to convert all prices to common units (in this instance £/Kg.) so that comparisons between suppliers can be made both in terms of single items and total purchases. It is emphasised that no account has been taken of viability of each sample. The unit value represents, within the limits already indicated, the actual costs per individual seed and gives a comparison between species as to their relative expense.

	Dkr/Kg	£/Kg @12.00	F.F./Kg	£/Kg @9.00	Fl./Kg	£/Kg @5.40	DM/Kg	£/Kg @5.00	£/lb	£/Kg	£/Kg	£/Kg	Mean Price £/Kg	Seed count ,000s/Kg	Unit of mean Value
Abies															
1. *A. cephalonica*	105	8.75	61	6.80	50	9.25	45	9.00	2.70	6.00	7.50	7.50	7.90	18.0	.044
2. *A. Koreana*	350	27.50	217	24.10	170	31.65	150	30.00	9.00	19.80	23.00	23.00	26.00	200.00	.013
3. *A. procera*	265	22.00	262	29.10	200	37.00	140	28.00	6.60	14.50	21.00	21.00	25.30	25.00	.011
4. *A. veitchii*	445	37.00	396	44.00	200	37.00	210	42.00	13.50	29.70	38.50	38.50	36.00	110.0	.033
Prunus															
5. *P. avium*	45	3.80	17	1.90	38	6.40	32	6.40	1.20	2.65	2.50	2.50	3.85	5.5	.070
6. *P. cerasifera*	12.50	1.00	12	1.30	10	1.10	5.5	1.10	0.35	0.75	4.00	4.00	1.70	2.0	0.85
7. *P. padus*	N/A	N/A	N/A	N/A	150	29.00	145	29.00	N/A	23.00 / N/A	23.00	23.00	26.60	15.0	.177
Total 1-6		100.05		107.20		122.40		114.50		73.40	96.50	96.50	100.85		
Total 1-7		—		—		151.40		143.50		—	119.50	119.50	127.45		

69

Appendix 6

Collection and Extraction of Seeds

The collection of seed may, on superficial examination, appear to be a reasonably simple operation: however as might be anticipated there are many possible problems associated with the successful gathering of the required material. Obviously many seeds or fruits can be dealt with relatively easily either by picking from the plant while standing at or about ground level or by picking up the dispersed material from the ground after it has been shed. Seeds such as acorns, conkers and Monkey Puzzle fruits are readily picked up by hand individually because of their sufficient size. Slightly smaller seeds such as Beechmast, Stone Pine and Maple seeds for example are marginally too small to be picked up individually unless cheap, efficient labour is available, but it can be brushed into heaps, shovelled up and separated from husk, scale and other detritus by winnowing or flotation in water.

Fruits of leguminous subjects are most readily collected before the pods explode and disperse the seeds, extraction can then be carried out under controlled conditions so that the seeds are not scattered beyond collection. Similarly coniferous subjects are most satisfactorily collected just prior to the cones opening and liberating their seeds — so that again this can be done under artificial conditions and the seed collected safely: however care should be exercised when drying cones of some species as desiccation of the actual seeds themselves may prove to be detrimental (e.g. *Abies).*

Berried fruits are usually fairly readily picked from the plant but in common with 'nut' type seeds they present a short term problem of 'heating' when kept in bulk, it is important therefore to remove field heat quickly by hydro-cooling and then store as cool as possible in small units. The same problem arises with seed which is collected 'green' and has to be held for a short period while it is cleaned, assessed and prepared.

One of the remaining problems is the extraction of the seeds or stony part of the fruit from the flesh of 'berry' type fruits such as Roses,Thorns, Rowans, Barberries, Cherries, etc. so that in those cases where the pulp produces a germination inhibitor this is removed and in addition the 'seeds' can be more easily handled and managed. The process must involve the necessity for separating the seeds from the pulp and skin of the fruit. This can be achieved in a number of ways, *viz:-*

i) warm temperature stratification so that the flesh is simply rotted off: it may also have a useful side effect of reducing a hard seedcoat but presents the problem of separating the seeds from the medium for counting, and assessment.

Sorbus cuspidata
a uniform stand of seedlings at an ideal density, continuous leaf cover reduces the chances of annual weed infestation.

Alnus glutinosa
a uniform stand of seedlings early in the season which still have a fair amount of growth to make.

Nothofagus obliqua
an even stand of seedlings, both to the sides and end of the bed. Uniform development indicates good husbandry.

Nothofagus procera
an even stand of seedlings showing uniform development.

Ligustrum vulgare
an even stand of seedlings at approaching an ideal plant population. By this stage there is more or less a complete foliage cover.

Silver Fir
an even and regular stand of seedlings down and across the seedbed: adequate irrigation has also produced good flushing of growth.

Fraxinus excelsior / Berberis darwinii / Acer platanoides
an indication of the variety of species which will occur in adjacent beds: in this case dictated by similar treatments which required sowing at the same time.

Larch
an irregular stand caused by seed drifting in the wind at sowing time.

Shading

not generally necessary under British conditions but used in this case to prevent undue drying and temperature build up in a summer sown crop.

Gleditsia triacanthos

a poor crop due in this case to a cold and wet season, Gleditsia requires a warm season for successful germination.

Lawson's Cypress
an example of the losses which can be caused by 'Damping Off' diseases at emergence.

Bird Protection
it is sometimes necessary to protect seeds against birds, not necessarily because they eat the seeds but because they bath in the grit or fine tilth. Note also the mousetrap in the foreground.

Irrigation
the provision of sufficient water requires a semi permanent arrangement.

Irrigation
a detail of a particular layout.

Irrigation
the provision of water at any time is an important criterion of success in seedling production: for this purpose a sufficient reserve is essential.

Alnus
the patchiness of this crop was caused by drying at a critical phase during germination; there being insufficient water pressure to achieve cover at the top of the slope.

Sorbus aria
a plant whose growth rate is affected notoriously by drying and wetting: an example of undue drying which has prevented many seedlings from producing a second flush of growth so producing an uneven crop.

Raised seedbeds
an indication of the size and levels of raised seedbeds, especially useful on heavier soils for winter drainage.

Windbreaks
the use of netting to provide an immediately local reduction in windspeed.

Windbreaks
Alders being established to provide a windbreak, as a general rule they do not harbour important pests and diseases and so do not act as a reservior of infection.

ii) maceration of the fruits and flotation of the pulp and skins: this works well for *Cotoneaster* and *Aronia* where the seeds separate readily from the flesh.

iii) maceration, fermentation and flotation of the scum containing flesh and skins: this technique is necessary for those fruits in which some flesh adheres to the seeds or in which there is a large pulp to seed ratio.

iv) digestion with dilute inorganic acid: this system is used extensively for tomato seed extraction and the same technique can be used (see M.A.F.F. Bull. *77* 'Tomatoes').

The actual equipment needed for picking and collecting will obviously depend on the quantities required and the subjects to be tackled. Apart from suitable sized buckets, bags, sacks, etc. Apple picking bags have proved useful. Dealing with subjects of tree size however presents problems of actually physically getting to the seeds: in forestry practice seed is often available during felling operations but this is not practicable for ornamental subjects! Special equipment to reach such material is therefore a necessity especially with those conifers which produce cones at the crown. Although ladders will have an obvious place they have limitations in mobility over a tree, perhaps the most useful pieces of equipment are extending platforms such as are used to service lamp standards and trolleybus wires, at intermediate levels fork lift apparatus or tractor mounted fore-end loaders have been used effectively, but inevitably the equipment used will be a function of availability and cost.

Many fruits and seeds are taken by animals (especially squirrels) and birds, and it is prudent to give prioity to the collection of those subjects which are vulnerable to these agencies.

PART II

Encyclopaedic List of Genera

ABIES

The 'Silver Firs' constitute a genus of Conifers which has, in general terms, adapted particularly well to conditions in the British Isles, indeed *Abies grandis* and *Abies procera (Abies nobilis)* have established so successfully that they have been used to some advantage as forest trees. Under normal conditions they are quick growing, shapely and ornamental trees; however some species from China, the Himalayas, and the southern parts of northern America are not invariably successful. Many of these species have not established well in certain parts of this country because of the susceptibility of their early flushing growth to damage by late spring frosts, and the almost annual check to growth which this entails.

The female cones are produced and held in an upright fashion on the branches during the spring and these mature to the seed dispersal stage in the autumn of the same year. At dispersal the seeds are liberated by the disintegration of the cone scales from the central axis of the cone, which still remains attached to the tree. Fertile seeds are generally not produced at the end of the cone.

The cones should be collected just prior to that stage at which they break up in order to facilitate the extraction of the seed. It is necessary to exercise care in extracting the seeds as they are soft, thin coated and somewhat oily, they are easily damaged both by drying and mechanical action. The cones are best broken up after a period of sun drying in a cold glasshouse, when they have been brought to the disintegration stage. Attempts to de-wing the seed by mechanical methods will usually damage the seed.

Because of its soft, thin coated constitution, the seed deteriorates rapidly in conventional dry storage, seeds of most of the species declining to a virtual complete loss of viability within twelve months, *Abies concolor* is particularly susceptible to desiccation under these conditions. Some success can be achieved by moisture controlled storage at cold (1-3°C) temperatures, viability being maintained at acceptable levels for 3 to 4 years with some species, *Abies grandis* has proved particularly adaptable to this regime.

Abies, like *Cedrus* and *Picea,* does not store well and because of the constitution of the seed with its thin coat and oily food reserve they are particularly easily infected by fungi, which may cause seed rots in all but ideal storage conditions.

73

The literature suggests that very often, and especially in years of light crops, the seed is infested by *Megastigmus* flies, but in the United Kingdom outside the forest situation, it does not seem to be of any great significance.

The Silver Firs are relatively unusual amongst the Conifers in that most seed samples contain a considerable proportion of seeds with a physiological embryo dormancy. The embryos of these seeds require a period of exposure to cold temperature (albeit relatively short) before germination will occur. It is therefore the practice to sow the seeds of this genus as soon after collection as possible so that the necessary chilling treatment is catered for in the seed-bed, at the same time providing suitable conditions for the maintenance of the viability at its highest reasonable level and avoiding the necessity for short term storage. Should it be necessary to spring sow then germination is considerably enhanced by chilling the imbibed seeds for 21 days at 3°C prior to sowing and this may prove a particularly useful technique for commercial samples received in the spring.

The seeds are sown broadcast in the conventional manner with a view to producing a population of about 500 per square metre.

The seedlings are prone to 'Damping Off' and suitable treatment to control this is an essential feature in the production of this genus. They may also be subject to attack by *Adelges* in the seedbed but the use of a suitable systemic insecticide will normally control an infestation.

The literature suggests that seedlings of *Abies* are susceptible to bright sunlight in the seedling year and that some form of light shade may be worth-while, however, British experience suggests that in most years the value of shade on a few exceptionally bright days (which in fact may do no harm) is more than offset by the reduction in growth caused by a low photosynthetic activity during the remainder of the season.

In forestry practice Silver Fir seedlings are usually left in the seedbed for two years (2 + 0) to reach a usable size, but those which are required for ornamental purposes should receive a sufficiently improved husbandry in nursery practice to allow removal at the end of the first year.

The chief problem associated with the seedling production of this genus in nursery practice is assessing the value of bought-in seed from commercial sources as the standard patterns of extraction from the cone, seed treatment and storage conditions produce such considerable impacts that the viability of seed samples varies quite dramatically.

Seedlings of the species of Silver Fir are chiefly grown on, either as open ground or container grown for use as ornamental specimens. In a few cases seedlings are potted for use as rootstocks for the propagation by grafting of the hybrids, varieties, etc. which must be produced vegetatively and are not readily produced from cuttings. If seedlings are to be grown on, under glass or polythene the Silver Firs are particularly susceptible to infestation by Red Spider Mite, which however are not normally a problem in the open ground seedbed.

The seed count in this genus is remarkably variable depending markedly on the degree to which the sample has been dried, the source of the sample and the particular year of harvest. It is exceedingly difficult to derive consistent figures as the variations in seed count for this genus are such that 74 the highest counts for a particular species may be twice the lowest.

ASSOCIATED READING

Heit, C.E. (1968) 'Propagation from seed 14: Testing and growing less common and exotic fir species', Amer. Nurs. *127* (10) : 10.

Species	Seedcount in 1,000s/kg		
	Source 1	Source 2	Author
A. cephalonica	+	15.6	23.0
A. cilicica	+	10.0	10.5
A. concolor	24.0	28.0	24.5
A. firma	+	+	25.0
A. fraseri	123.0	128.5	130.0
A. grandis	51.0	42.0	25.0
A. homolepis	+	61.6	49.0
A. kawakamii	+	+	54.0
A. koreana	+	+	200.0
A. lasiocarpa	82.5	77.0	81.0
A. magnifica	14.5	18.7	16.0
A. nordmannianna	+	17.0	18.5
A. pindrow	+	+	+
A. pinsapo	+	+	25.0
A. procera (nobilis)	32.0	23.5	24.0
A. veitchii	+	132.0	100.0

This comparison of seedcounts has been derived from the average figures from two reliable sources and from limited data derived by the author from samples obtained during the 1973 to 1975 seasons. The figures are presented in order to demonstrate the variation which occurs, as well as indicating to the propagator the relative seed size of each species.

ACER

The Maples are one of the largest and most diverse of woody plant genera which are included in these notes, the genus contains a great many species; Hillier lists more than seventy five which gives some indication of the number of species in cultivation, although somewhat less than half this number are at all commonly encountered. The species vary from large forest trees such as the 'Sycamore' (*Acer pseudoplatanus)* and *Acer opalus* to fairly small shrubby subjects such as *Acer ginnala, Acer japonicum* and *Acer palmatum*. Geographically the genus is mostly native to the north temperate regions of the world and the wide variety and number of species means that at least one will be found in almost any area of this zone.

The majority of Maples have some distinctive ornamental or decorative value while a few are amongst the most outstanding ornamental subjects in bark and leaf of all hardy woody plants. The potential of some of the north american natives in terms of autumn colour is phenomenal, for it is these few species which form the basis of 'fall colour' in eastern North America. The greater proportion of species thrive in the British climate although the cultivation of a limited number is determined by soil type and the incidence 75 of spring frost. Because of the diversity and number of species involved in nursery production it is inevitable that some species will be grown for root-stock purposes, either for other, sufficiently closely related and compatible, species of which seed is not easily obtainable; or for the wide range of variants which are a feature of some species *viz. Acer palmatum* and *Acer platanoides.* The complexities and likely compatibilities of various inter-relationships concerning this facet have been discussed.

The fruit of the Maple is a one seeded winged samara: in most cases flowering is in spring and the fruit matures in the autumn and is dispersed quickly. Exceptionally, flowering is earlier with a mid-summer dispersal and immediate germination. The seed is generally short lived which is a characteristic of genera such as this, which predominantly store their food as lipids, there is consequently a difficult storage problem in the long term.

The majority of species do not present any difficulties in seedling production although all species which exhibit autumn dispersal show some form of dormancy control. Most have a cold temperature, embryo type dormancy but a few species additionally develop a hard seedcoat condition, either naturally or as a result of drying in artificial storage, and this prevents germination occuring until the second spring after dispersal.

Those species developing hard seedcoats tend to dry their fruit more extensively before dispersal. Dry storage of Maple seeds can have disastrous effects in terms of viability and this accounts for the failures of many samples of seed, from commercial sources, to germinate. Marginal drying may not cause complete loss of viability but it may enhance the development of a hard seedcoat which may not otherwise naturally occur. In the British Isles seeds of the following alien species usually develop a hard seedcoat condition if left until dispersal:- *Acer capillipes, Acer pensylvanicum, Acer rufinerve, Acer ginnala, Acer tartaricum, Acer japonicum, Acer griseum and Acer nikoense. Acer campestre* (the native 'Field Maple') also exhibits this condition. In order to overcome the need for stratification or to overcome the delayed germination, it is relatively easy to avoid this dormancy by collecting the seed 'green' and sowing immediately. In this way the seed is sown before the development of the hard seedcoat and further hardening is prevented by the moist situation in the seedbed. Embryo chilling to overcome dormancy is achieved in the sedbed over winter, with germination occurring in the spring. It is difficult to describe an exact and easily identifiable 'green' condition for such a wide range of species. In most cases collection when the wings of the fruit are yellow-brown in colour is the best guide, although this condition occurs at different periods for the various species, it does however allow some flexibility, as this condition extends over a period of about three weeks, prior to the 'drying phase', which is the condition to be avoided.

Storage in this condition, of course, is not feasible if only because of the heating which would occur.

Normally *Acer pseudoplatanus, Acer trautvetteri, Acer platanoides, Acer palmatum, Acer opalus, Acer crataegifolium, Acer davidii, Acer grosseri, Acer hersii and Acer macrophyllum* only develop an embryo dormancy condition which merely requires a winter's chilling for after-ripening, although in some species a hard seedcoat condition can be induced by drying and this is often apparent in commercial samples of *Acer*

palmatum.

Acer rubrum and *Acer sacharinum* both mature their seeds in early summer and ideally they should be sown immediately at dispersal before any further drying occurs, under these conditions germination will be rapid and uniform. The literature tends to suggest that the vitality of the seeds of these two species is transient, but successful storage of *Acer rubrum* especially has been achieved for periods of up to twelve months if processed when fresh, kept sealed and stored at low temperature. The viability of most species is very good and can readily be assessed by a cutting test; the exception is, of course, *Acer griseum* which often shows very reduced proportion of sound embryos — for a variety of reasons, chief of which are frost and the sex of the flowers. *Acer negundo* has the same problem, but because it is dioecious.

Sowing involves the distribution of the complete fruit, usually with the wing attached, as it is difficult to remove the wings satisfactorily in a 'green' condition. The 'seed' is sown on a conventional seedbed and broadcast to produce a population of 250 per square metre for the larger growing subjects. Maples benefit from a seedbed with a high level of leaf litter, peat etc. which produces a noticeably more fibrous root system and aids transplanting.

No detailed data has been presented on seedcounts because accuracy in this aspect will only be achieved with dry and de-winged fruits and as dried seed is of low viability it has only academic interest. Seed is recommended to be collected 'green' and the count will obviously vary considerably with the moisture content; however a table is appended indicating counts made at a suitable 'green' stage but is only intended as a guide.

Seed from commercial sources may well have developed some degree of hard seedcoat and in extreme cases may require stratification for a year prior to sowing but in some more marginal cases it may be overcome by a 48 hour warm water soak prior to early sowing.

The seedlings of Maple tend to germinate early and if seed is stratified, chitting may occur in the bin unless sowing is sufficiently early. Because of this habit emergence is early and the seedlings are exposed to frost. They are very susceptible to damage or even death at this stage unless protection is provided.

Under normal circumstances Maple seedlings do not suffer from any particular attacks of pests or diseases although they may be beset by such general problems as aphids and 'damping off'.

A number of species (especially those in the *Negundo* section of the genus) are dioecious and all samples of fruit should be checked to ensure that fruits do contain a seed and viable embryo. Some species, especially those in the *Acer grosseri, Acer hersii, Acer davidii* group hybridise and in many cases the parent plants are of hybrid origin, consequently all possible parent trees should be progeny tested to assess their value in producing true to name seedlings.

ASSOCIATED READING

Anderson,N.A. (1970) 'Propagating *Acer palmatum* by seed'. The Plant Prop.*16* (4):5.

Curtis, W.J. (1969) 'Seed germination and culture of *Acer palmatum*'. Proc.Int. Plant

Prop. Soc. *19*: 142.

Fordham,A.J. (1969) *'Acer griseum* and its propagation', Proc.Int
Plant Prop.Soc. *19*:346.

Hadfield, M. (1970) 'Raising Maples from Seed', Gard. Chron. *168* (6): 26

Hadfield,M. (1971) 'Raising Maples from Seed', Gard. Chron. *169* (8): 54

Harris, J. (1971) 'Raising Maples from Seed', Gard. Chron. *170* (1) : 25

Hutchinson, P.A. (1971) 'Propagation of Acers from Seed', Proc. Int.
Plant Prop. Soc. *21*: 233.

McMillan Browse, P.D.A. (1971) 'Propagation of some acers'. Gard.
Chron. *169* (22): 25.

Nordine, R.M.(1962) 'Collection, storage and germination of Maple seed', Proc.
Plant Prop. Soc. *2* : 62.

Vertrees, J.D. (1972) 'Observations on the propagation of asiatic maples'. Proc.
Int. Plant Prop. Soc. *22*: 192.

Wells.J.S. (1968) 'Plant Propagation Practices', Macmillan, N.Y., 3rd Ed.

Dormancy conditions encountered in the more commonly cultivated species of Acer.

1. Species which exhibit only embryo dormancy under normal conditions and require a winter's chilling to germination.

    AA. crataegifolium* davidii*, distylum*, grosseri*, hersii*, macrophyllum, mono, monspessulanum, opalus*, palmatum*, platanoides, pseudoplatanus, saccharum, trautvetteri;

    * species which develop a hard seedcoat with a period of dry storage.

2. Species which exhibit no dormancy controls:— *AA. rubrum, saccharinum* and *A. pycnanthum.*

3. Species which normally develop a hard seedcoat and exhibit embryo dormancy:— *AA. campestre, capillipes, circinatum,[+] ginnala,[+], griseum, japonicum, nikoense, pensylvanicum,[+] rufinerve,[+] tartaricum.[+]* Occasionally samples of seed from species marked [+] will not produce a sufficiently hard seedcoat to delay germination.

Seed counts in various species of Acer at the 'green' collection stage.

Species	Seeds/kg
A. campestre	5,500
A. griseum	4,000
A. grosseri	35,000
A. pensylvanicum	28,000
A. platanoides	4,000
A. pseudoplatanus	7,000

AESCULUS

The 'Horse Chestnuts' and 'Buckeyes' are readily produced from seed and in those situations where seed can be obtained locally or is available from commercial sources, this system of propagation ultimately produces the most reliable specimens. However, availability of seed is such that, usually all but the common types have to be propagated by vegetative means. Normally vegetative propagation of these subjects is achieved by some form of working onto a rootstock and suitability of available sorts for use as rootstocks should be considered.

Ae hippocastanum — the 'Horse Chestnut' sets good crops of seed each year. The tree is, of course, common in most lowland areas of the British Isles and availability is not a limiting factor. Seed size can be very variable from year to year viz. between 100-200 seeds per kilogram and it is therefore important to assess this early in the collection, so that sufficient numbers can be collected. In 1975, which was an exceptionally good summer, the nuts were very large at 55 per kilogram.

Ae. indica — the 'Indian Horse Chestnut' sets good seed in most years but because of its relatively late flowering habit the season for seed development is short and therefore in dull seasons, i.e. low light intensity, the size of the seed may be quite small, this does not appear to affect viability but obviously limits the resource of the seed in supporting seedling growth. The tree is not uncommon in larger parks and gardens in England.

Ae. x carnea — the 'Red Horse Chestnut', although of hybrid origin this tree has at some stage doubled its chromosome content and as a result of tetraploidy is capable of producing viable seed which comes reasonably true to type. Seed is set in most years but production of good crops is periodic, the seeds only maturing to a usable stage in response to a good summer. In dull years the seeds are small, white or blotched white with a milky inside and in this condition are valueless. The tree is a relatively common subject both in parks and gardens and occasionally in farmland. Normally sound seed weights are around 200 to 250 to the kilogram, but in 1975 it was as low as 100 per kilogram.

Ae. flava (octandra) — the 'Yellow Buckeye' or 'Sweet Buckeye' sets seed periodically in response to a good summer. Seeds from English sources are small in size but produce satisfactory trees. It is not encountered frequently in the U.K. but can be found in many of the parklands in the south of England.

Ae. pavia — the 'Red Buckeye' is rarely seen in the U.K. and plants purporting to be this species should be scrutinised carefully as the majority of specimens are of hybrid origin. Unless the parent can be positively indentified the seed should be regarded as of spurious value.

Ae. turbinata — the 'Japanese Horse Chestnut' is not commonly encountered in the U.K. as it is fairly close to the Horse Chestnut in form and appearance. It is climatically suited to conditions in this country and sets good crops of seed in most years.

Ae. californica and *Ae. glabra* are uncommon in the U.K. but set seed in hot, bright summers.

Periodicity of seed production in this group of plants does not appear to be of regular frequency but is influenced for the most part by the nature of the growing season each year. Many of the American species only seem to set seed crops of good quality in seasons which experience high light intensities and summer temperatures which presumably approach conditions in their native habitat.

As only *Ae. hippocastanum* and *Ae. x carnea* are usually available from   79 the commercial seedhouses, it is necessary to locate mature seed bearing trees of the other species to obtain supplies.

In order to achieve the most effective results, the seed of these trees should be collected as soon as it is shed and sown with the minimum of delay, so that no further drying occurs.

After collection the seed can be conveniently sorted by flotation in water, satisfactory viable seed sinks while void, infested and damaged seed floats. The seeds should not be kept in bulk for too long, after collection unless they are quickly cooled as they are prone to heat up quickly and this will inevitably damage the embryo.

Seeds of this genus store much of their foods as lipids and in consequence degenerate rapidly on drying both in terms of viability loss and the deterioration of stored food. Loss of quality in this respect can be recognised externally by dull, dry and ultimately wrinkled seedcoats, and internally by the progressive development of brown necrotic areas throughout the tissue of the seed. The successful maintenance of quality can be recognised by the retention of the waxy, polished appearance of the seed.

The viability of imported seed is usually poor because the seed has been subjected to a degree of drying as a result of storage and transportation. However existing vigour can be retained and any further loss arrested if the seed is soaked for twenty-four hours in warm water and then sown.

In order to store seed effectively it is important to start with a freshly collected sample when viability and quality are at their highest level. Storage is achieved by sealing in a polythene bag to conserve high humidity and keeping at between 1 and 3°C. If it is suspected that fungal rots will be troublesome the seed can be dressed with a suitable fungicide. Under these conditions adequate levels of viability and vigour can be maintained for twelve months and some use for two years.

Short term storage from collection until spring sowing is satisfactorily achieved by placing the seeds in boxes with damp peat and keeping in a cold place.

As the seeds are large they can be space sown at a predetermined density and with an expected maximum germination response, this is the same as seedling density - the large seedeness effectively meaning no field losses.

Experience has shown that populations of between 150 and 175 seedlings per square metre provides maximum productivity. This is achieved by a spacing of ± 8cm by ± 8 cm.

Chestnuts are not usually susceptible to pests and diseases in the seedbed other than the occasional infestations by cut worm. Seeds may be lost from the seedbed as a result of the predations of rodents, crows etc. but this can be discouraged by tainting the seed with paraffin prior to sowing. In areas which are susceptible to late spring frosts, it is advisable to provide the seedlings with some protection, for although the seedlings are rarely killed outright by frosts they can be severely checked in their growth and may lose their growing point. This will affect the ultimate size and quality of the one year old seedling.

Seedlings may be used simply as field liners for growing on as specimen trees in their own right or may be used to provide rootstocks for varieties, hybrids and for the species of which seed is not obtainable. Traditionally *Ae. hippocastanum* has been solely used as a rootstock because of its ready availability. However it is not entirely satisfactory for the less vigorous types because of the large and unsightly overgrowth which occurs at the union. Some assessment should therefore be made of the suitability of stock/scion combinations and some extension of range be introduced — even if *Ae. x carnea* only is used as an alternative for less vigorous subjects, it as least has the virtue that if field working fails that the rootstock may be grown on in its own right and prove a more valuable investment than the common 'Horse Chestnut'.

SUITABLE STOCK/SCION RELATIONSHIPS FOR AESCULUS

Rootstock	Suitable scion groups
Ae. x carnea	var. 'Brioti', *Ae. flava*, *Ae. x plantierensis*
Ae. flava	*Ae. pavia* hybrids and less vigorous types
Ae. hippocastanum	vars., + *dallimorei*, *Ae. indica* and vars, *Ae. turbinata*
Ae. indica	var. 'Sydney Pearce'
Ae. pavia	small growing hybrids from south-eastern States

In order to produce rootstocks for budding in the first summer after germination, the following procedure should be adopted. The seed is chilled, germinated and the radicle pinched, it is then sown at the required spacing in the field. This technique has been used successfully in Holland but its use in the U.K. would probably be limited by soil conditions. Currently treatment of the growing tip of the seedling with Gibberellic Acid has produced big enough stocks for budding.

Ae. parviflora - this shrubby Buckeye from the south-eastern United States only sets seed in this country in very hot and late summers e.g. 1959, conventionally it is vegetatively propagated by root cuttings.

However, information from the U.S. (Fordham 1973), suggests that this species exhibits epicotyl dormancy when grown from seed. If seed is available for propagation then this phenomenon should be expected.

ASSOCIATED READING

Fordham, A.J. (1973) 'Dormancy in seeds of temperate woody plants', Proc. Int. Plant Prop. Soc. *23* : 262.

AILANTHUS

The only species of this genus usually found in cultivation in the British Isles is the chinese 'Tree of Heaven' *(A. altissima/ A. glandulosa)*. Normally this tree is propagated vegetatively by root cuttings, as the species is dioecious and as the male plant emits an offensive odour at flowering it is considered undesirable.

Seed is not normally produced by trees in this country but it is readily available each year from normal commercial sources and obtaining it is not a problem.

The winged fruit is usually fairly small and dried, and although much of the seed is apparently sound, germination rates of viable seeds can be as low as 30% or less even under good seedbed conditions.

The seed germinates quite satisfactorily under cool glasshouse conditions which suggests that the seed does not exhibit any dormancy conditions. Indeed there appears to be no problem in this respect but in common with many other subjects of more southerly temperate distribution the level and vigour of germination is usually enhanced by exposure of the seed to only a limited period of chilling prior to germination.

Seed should therefore be sown in the late winter or early spring to cater for this situation: sowing is by broadcasting the seed at a rate determined so as to produce a population of about 300 per square metre.

No problems have been encountered in the seedbed, albeit only from limited experience.

Species	Seedcount ,000s/kg
A. altissima	15.0

ALNUS

The three species of Alders, now well naturalised in the British Isles (*A. cordata, A. glutinosa* and *A.incana)* have not been as extensively planted during the last decade as might have been forecast. The recommendation that they should be more normally used for windbreak planting especially around orchards has not produced the expected demand, despite their freedom from hosting pests and diseases of fruit which bedevils the use of Poplars and Plums. This trend led to an increase in production which now appears to be declining. However, with the trend towards more natural plantings in the landscape both in the urban situation and on motorway verges it is possible to visualise a renewal of interest in these subjects especially in the damper sites.

The various ornamental forms of Alder maintain a steady demand and although these can fairly readily be produced from cuttings it is conventional nursery practice to produce these among the field tree crops and they are produced by working onto a rootstock.

Thus there continues to be a continued interest for the production of Alders for these two purposes.

The seeds of Alders are produced in strobiles or cones in much the same way as their near relatives the Birches. However, they differ quite distinctly in that the cones of Birch break up to liberate the fruits whereas the cones of Alder open on the tree and the fruits are shaken out by wind. The 'seeds' are in effect small winged fruits and dispersal begins when they are ripe, but this process tends to continue well into winter as the cones slowly open. Collecting the seeds is therefore a question of picking the cones just as they begin to change colour and open, so that the seeds can be shaken out after a period of drying. The traditional system is to cut branches of cones which are hung up to dry and are then shaken at intervals. This latter system saves the bother of having to separate the seeds from the cone material if they are simply dried and broken up.

The seeds are very similar to those of Birch and are small and light. Once sown these thin coated seeds have a low survival rate and it is therefore necessary to modify the Field Factor accordingly when calculating sowing rates.

Although dry storage is normally the practice, these relatively small thin coated seeds tend to deteriorate quickly and show a marked decline in viability. Moist cool storage however is equally difficult as the seed easily becomes waterlogged and the seeds are prone to rotting.

Autumn sowing provides the best conditions for seed survival and the maintenance of acceptable levels of viability, although it may be early winter before the cones are sufficiently ripened and the seeds extracted.

As the seeds are small the seedbed should be prepared to a fine tilth prior to sowing. The seed is sown broadcast and then firmed in to ensure contact with the soil and avoid bounce when covered. Covering is with grit in the conventional fashion. The difficulty in assessing the field factor accurately often means that the crop is thicker than anticipated and thinning at an early stage may be necessary.

The dormancy conditions of Alders appear to be of the cold temperature embryo type although it would appear that some samples and portions of some samples do not develop dormancy conditions. However, the majority of available evidence and observation suggests that both germination level and germination rates are profoundly improved if the seed is exposed to a period of chilling prior to subjecting it to suitable conditions for germination.

Seed rates should be assessed with a view to producing 200 to 250 seedlings per square metre.

The seedlings will inevitably be affected by low temperatures in the spring and although Alders are hardy subjects some protection against frost should be provided.

Pest and disease incidence on Alders in the seedbed is remarkably low and it would appear that routine spraying will control any likely infection.

Seeds of Alder, although similar to Birch, are relatively much heavier (although still small), seedcounts however are of little value as the proportion of empty and unsuitable material varies considerably from year to year.

Species	Seedcount ,000s/kg	Annual Variation	
A. cordata	800	)	
A. glutinosa	750	)	±20%
A. incana	1,000	)	

AMELANCHIER

This rosaceous genus (closely related to *Aronia*) chiefly of north american trees and shrubs are variously known as the 'Snowy Mespilus', 'June Berry', 'Service Berry' and 'Shad Bush', reflecting in terms of common names the confusion which exists in their scientific description. They are extremely closely allied in their characters which make them difficult to distinguish and also makes them prone to hybridisation in cultivation. It is therefore important to obtain seed from a single species group, preferably from a natural stand. However if seed can be reliably collected from a local source then this may enhance successful germination.

The species are, in the main, early spring flowering with the consequent fruit production in mid-summer. The fruit is a small fleshy, typical pome and is often abundantly produced if climatic conditions at fertilisation are not untoward.

If the seed can be extracted at this stage and sown without drying, germination will usually occur the following spring. The fruits must be watched and collected without delay when ripe, as they are very attractive to birds who will completely strip a tree or bush very quickly at this stage. The fruits simply need maceration and then the seeds can be collected by floating the skins and pulp in water.

If the seed is bought in as dried berries or seed, the seedcoat has usually hardened by this stage and germination will be delayed by twelve months while this condition is reduced. Imported seed is therefore normally warm stratified for one season prior to a winter's chilling to overcome embryo dormancy. If dried seed was obtainable in late summer a warm followed by a cold artificial treatment would overcome the problem and permit germination during the first spring.

This genus does not commonly develop any particular problems in the seedbed. Seedling populations will vary according to the vigour and stature of the particular species grown but will generally be about 250 to 300 per square metre.

Species	Seedcount in ,000s/kg
A. canadensis	210
A. ovalis	125

ARAUCARIA

The Monkey Puzzle (*A. araucaria*) is the only species of this genus which is at all commonly encountered in the British Isles, for it is the only one which has proved sufficiently hardy to withstand the vagaries of climatic conditions in the more exposed areas. The less hardy species will occasionally thrive in the more favoured and milder parts of the country.

There are many mature seed bearing trees of the Monkey Puzzle around the countryside, for as a tree it was widely favoured and planted by our Victorian forebears. It would be prudent to collect seed from local trees as they have a proven hardiness and may well produce hardier seedlings than those derived from commercial seed samples, which will usually have originated in southern Europe and which may well prove to be more tender and be less reliable in the establishment period.

Normally the species is dioecious with separate male and female plants but occasionally specimens carrying both male and female flowers are encountered. The seed bearing cones are fertilised in mid-summer but the cones do not mature and shed their seeds until the autumn of the succeeding year or even the following one. Once it reaches a seed bearing condition a tree will normally produce regular crops thus obviating the necessity for any long term storage. Observations since its original introduction suggests that under normal conditions a well grown specimen will be seeding prolifically after about 30 years.

The seeds are fatty and do not maintain good levels of viability when dried, consequently they should be prevented from drying during the period from dispersal to sowing. The individual seeds are large, being 2.5 to 4 cm in length, and basically conical in shape with a rudimentary wing-like appendage at the broad end. They are shed from the tree in late September to October and can be readily collected from the ground. Being large seeds they can easily be sorted through on an individual basis in order to select for soundness, to clean the sample and to dewing in order to facilitate sowing. Seed from the commercial seedhouses is purchased on a seedcount rather than the conventional weight basis and is usually priced per 100 seeds.

Species	No. of seeds/kg.	Source
A. araucaria	300-400	U.K.

Although it is not usually necessary to store seed on the nursery, there is virtually no published information on suitable treatment. Deduction, however, would suggest that it would probably survive best if sealed in a fresh condition in a polythene bag and stored at a temperature of 1 to 3°C. This treatment would probably preserve an adequate degree of viability for one, or possibly, two years.

The seeds are sown onto a conventional ameliorated soil seedbed and either broadcast or dibbled individually. If sown broadcast the seeds should be well pressed into the compost so that they are fully in contact and may take up water readily.

The quality of seedlings derived from such large seeds may well be affected by the orientation of the seed at sowing, observations indicate that this aspect is of little significance unless they are sown with the apex pointing upwards. It would appear that naturally seeds lie horizontally or with the pointed end downwards.

As the seeds do not exhibit any dormancy factor they should not be sown too early or the emerging seedlings will be subject to the dangers of radiation frost unless some protection is provided. Seedlings appear to be particularly sensitive to frost damage.

Although the seedlings produced are not large in relation to their initial seed size and food reserve they should not be overcrowded if they are to reach an acceptable height. A population of about 400 seedlings per square metre would appear to be a reasonable compromise. As the seeds are selected 85 individually at least an eighty per cent success should be anticipated. One year old seedlings should achieve a height of 12cm by the end of the growing season.

The chief problem associated with this type of subject in current systems of nursery practice is the handling of the seedlings from the open ground situation at the end of the growing season, and it may therefore prove more realistic to sow the seeds individually in pots in order to facilitate the subsequent handling of the seedlings. *Araucaria* seedlings appear to be particularly free from pests and diseases in The British Isles. In the seedbed they are unlikely to be troubled other than by the activities of *Rhizoctonia* as a 'Damping Off' effect in particularly bad years. Usually any significant level of infection will be averted if satisfactory and suitable systems of seedbed management are practiced.

ARONIA

This genus of only three species (*A. arbutifolia, A. melanocarpa* and *A. prunifolia)* of deciduous, suckering shrubs is native to the north American continent. The 'chokeberries' are medium sized shrubs grown for their corymbs of white flowers which are produced in the spring and their colourful berries and vivid foliage hues in the autumn. They constitute a genus which is, at present, strangely unknown, especially as their autumnal colouring does not appear to require acidic soil conditions. It is possible that they may become more in demand in the future with the trends to mass plantings in the urban landscape and along motorways.

In nursery practice the three species are usually propagated either by cuttings or more commonly by divisions of the suckering crown, but large scale production would be more realistic by seed. The fruits, which are fleshy pomes are very akin in shape to Rowan berries, are produced in the late summer and autumn. Those of *A. arbutifolia* and *A. prunifolia* persist well into the winter in this country for they are not among the first subjects to be stripped by birds; so that collection is not a critical problem. The fruits of *A. melanocarpa* however tend to drop very soon after they are ripened and collection does become critical. The berries of all three species may contain up to five seeds but under British climatic conditions rarely are more than two or three produced — the remainder aborting but still appearing as under sized seeds. The fruits are readily stripped from the bushes by hand.

The seeds are fairly easily extracted from the berries, the flesh and skin being somewhat insubstantial: so that following maceration the material should be agitated in water and the supernatant mixture decanted off successively, until only the seeds are left on the bottom. The seeds are relatively small compared with the size of fruits and although accurate records have not been kept, all three species weigh similarly, between five and six hundred thousand seeds per kilogramme.

Commercial seed is often offered as dried berries but the seeds can be extracted fairly readily by soaking and reconstituting, rubbing and separating as already described.

After extraction the seeds should be sufficiently dried so that they separate and run freely. In this state they are easily sown. Storage can be achieved by sealing in a jar at cool temperatures, for probably two years with adequate retention of viability.

The seeds exhibit a simple embryo dormancy which requires a period of chilling to overcome before germination will occur. The limited evidence available suggests that the amount of chilling required varies between the species. The recommendations for *A. arbutifolia* are 12 to 14 weeks at temperatures below 5°C, while *A. prunifolia* will respond at temperatures up to 10°C. However, winter stratification or autumn sowing will achieve the necessary end result.

Stratification of the berries has the advantage of eliminating the problem of extraction but it does pose the problem of separation from the medium for sowing and testing. The small seeds are particularly difficult to mix evenly with the medium if the sowing of the complete mixture is envisaged.

The seed is sown broadcast onto a normal prepared seedbed, firmed in and covered with grit. In assessing sowing rates it should be borne in mind that the seeds are small and if autumn sown have to survive the winter, so modifying the field factor element. Stratification does not necessarily reduce lossess because of the possibilities of localised waterlogging in the medium. A seedling population of about 300 per square metre produces seedlings of adequate size and vigour.

The seedlings are relatively hardy but sudden radiation frost will check them although not killing outright. Pests and diseases do not appear to raise any particular problems if routine schedules of spraying are adhered to through the growing season.

ASSOCIATED READING

Crocker, W. and L.V. Barton (1931) 'After ripening, germination and storage of certain rosaceous seeds', Contrib. Boyce Thompson Inst. *3* (3): 385.

BERBERIS

The Barberries are a large and diverse genus of both deciduous and evergreen shrubs, which are however remarkably similar in flower structure and fruiting habits. The flowers are typically produced in early summer and the berries mature in the autumn of the same year. In most species good crops of fruit are produced annually, and because of this habit of prolific seed production, and relative ease of germination, many Barberries are raised in this way. However seedling production in this genus should be subject to some caution and critical appraisal, before any particular species is raised from seed. Many species exhibit an unusual propensity to hybridise and some samples of seed from particular species are of spurious value if it is intended to produce the seedlings for distribution — a failing especially attributable to *B. darwinii* and *B. gagnepainii* — some progeny of these species being almost unrecognisable. However variation is of course acceptable in seed of 'Chinese Hybrids' etc. and seedlings will be expected to vary.

In effect the question posed for the seedling production of Barberries is an ethical one and devolves on the hybridity of the seed and the acceptability of the progeny as being typical.

B. julianae, B. vulgaris, B. thunbergii and *B. dictiophylla* can usually be relied upon to produce acceptably uniform and typical seedling stands. *B. vulgaris*, 'Foliis purpureis' is normally produced from seed for use as a rootstock for working the more difficult to vegetatively propagate species such as *B. dictiophylla* and its variants. *B. thunbergii 'Atropurpurea'* seeds can be obtained and will generally produce progeny of the type — although the ethics of labelling it 'Atropurpurea' which indicates vegetative origin is suspect, it is also possible to obtain seed of 'red' leaved variations from the United States which come true and produce very worthwhile plants.

Fruits can be collected locally quite readily but the likelihood of hybridization must be accounted for before any sample is used, and certainly samples from *B. darwinii* and *B. gagnepainii* should only be collected from fairly extensive, single species stands in which the parent plants are typical of the species, such as will occur in hedgerows etc.; *B. x stenophylla* is of hybrid origin and despite its prolific production of seed should not be propagated in this way. *B. julianae* and *B. dictiophylla* do not usually hybridise, for lack of suitably related species, and can be expected to be reliable. Because of these problems of variability it would be prudent to recommend that plants intended for specimen planting should be propagated vegetatively, and that only subjects intended for rootstocks, hedging or 'landscape' planting should be grown from seed unless the trueness to type of the sample is valid.

There are no real problems in general terms associated with the germination of Berberis seedlings. They exhibit a typical embryo dormancy requiring a limited period of chilling to overcome inhibition to germination but this is normally a relatively small effect so that late winter/early spring sowing is adequate to achieve a late spring/early summer germination.

Seed of a wide range of species is normally available from continental sources and in many instances this is offered as dried berries.

Clean seed can be obtained by macerating fresh berries, marginally fermenting and then floating off the pulp. This material should be sown broadcast in the conventional fashion. The sowing of the entire fruits should not delay germination as the pulp does not appear to develop any inhibitors to germination; but as the fruits may contain several seeds it produces a patchy emergence and an uneven grade out. Similarly if dried berries are obtained it is more realistic to try and reconstitute them by soaking so that the seeds can be extracted.

Berberis seedlings in general do not achieve great size in their seedling year and can be sown to produce a population of 450-500 per square metre.

The seedlings are particularly sensitive to damping off diseases in the seedbed and routine spray precautions are an essential feature of the production of this genus.

BETULA

Three species of Birch are native to the British Isles and the two tree types are commonly produced from seed; many alien species have, however, been successfully introduced and are well established as ornamental subjects in parks, gardens and arboreta.

In nursery practice most of the introduced tree species and their varieties are produced by grafting onto either of the two relevant native species. However, where seed is available trees of better quality and greater longevity are produced, but the effective success of this system is limited by the 'trueness-to-type' of the seedling population, as many vegetatively propagated forms have been selected for particular characteristics. (e.g. bark colour) and when grown from seed develop a range of these characteristics, this is especially true even with natural variants such as *Betula albo-sinensis septentrionalis*.

The seeds of Birch are produced in 'cones' which mature in the late autumn, these dry out and break up while still attached to the tree so that the seed is dispersed by wind. This habit causes obvious difficulties for the seed collector who must attempt to collect seed prior to cone disintegration. In practice it is possible to extract seed from the cones while they are still greenish, by spreading them to avoid heating and drying gently. The cones can then be rubbed to break them up, and the seed and scales can be partially separated by fanning; however the resultant sample still contains a fair proportion of cone material. When dealing with small quantities of alien species it is probably easiest to dry and break up the cone and sow the entire mixture of seed and cone scales.

Birch seed is thus not the easiest to deal with and seed counts must be made on a representative sample of the impure seed and the whole sample sown on this basis. As the seed of Birch is relatively small and thin coated, viability tends to deteriorate in storage and will deteriorate further after sowing by losses included within the field factor and this should be allowed for when assessing this aspect of the calculation.

In practice autumn sowing provides environmental conditions under which good levels of viability are maintained and germination levels and vigour are acceptable. The literature generally promotes confusion concerning the method of dealing with Birch at sowing especially in relation to the covering of the seed. Black and Wareing however have satisfactorily sorted out the problems for the native Birch, these species produce light sensitive seeds which under certain conditions will only germinate in the presence of light. The complexities of these requirements can be summarised as follows.

If the seeds are autumn sown and are adequately chilled in the seedbed over the winter then the seeds will germinate in the absence of light during the spring, in consequence the seed can be covered when sown.

Seeds sown and covered in the late winter early spring period which do not germinate because of inadequate chilling often do germinate late in the season if soil temperatures rise to the 25°C as they did in many seedbeds in 1975. Thus if spring germination of Birch seed fails then it may be prudent to cover the seedbed with glass lights to increase soil temperatures.

At intermediate temperatures and when the seed has not been chilled the seeds are light sensitive and should be sown, rolled in, but left uncovered so that they are exposed to light.

As the seeds are relatively small, the seedbed should be prepared to a fine tilth. The seeds are pressed in to make good contact with the soil and are then covered with grit. Traditional practice recommends that Birch seed should not be covered, but experience has shown that covering, at least with

89

grit, has no apparent detrimental effect on crop production as indicated above, unless spring sown.

Germination tends to occur early in the season and protection against spring frosts will be a necessity as seedlings of virtually all species will be susceptible.

Because of the difficulties encountered in making an accurate assessment of the field factor it is very possible that germination will be greater than anticipated and it will be necessary to thin the crop.

Birch seedlings are susceptible to 'Damping-off' diseases in the seedbed but routine precautions with a suitable copper spray should prevent excessive losses. The bud gall mite, *Eriophyes rudis,* particularly affects Birch in the seedbed and can be controlled by spraying with lime sulphur. A rust fungus, *Melampsoridium betulinum,* can cause premature defoliation of the seedlings with a consequent incomplete ripening of the wood and increased level of winter damage; all species, however, are not equally susceptible and *B. ermanii* and *B. utilis* are particularly resistant while *B. lutea, B. paprifera* and *B. japonica* are most resistant than the native species.

This system produces strong plants with good fibrous root systems at a population of 300-350 per square metre, which are suitable for field lining and quick establishment; seedlings for use as pot grown rootstocks will need to be smaller and should be produced at higher densities. *B. nigra* is an exceptional species in that it fruits and disperses its seeds in the early summer, if the seeds are collected and sown immediately then germination is good, even and prompt.

ASSOCIATED READING

Black, M. & P.F. Wareing (1959) 'The role of germination inhibitors and oxygen in the dormancy of light sensitive seeds of *Betula spp'*, J. Exp. Bot. *10*: 134

CALOCEDRUS

Virtually the only species of 'Incense Cedar' to be encountered in the British Isles is *C. (Libocedrus) decurrens* although it is not as widely planted as it might warrant.

Seed is readily obtained from commercial seed sources, although seed production in Britain is reasonably common if adequate sized mature specimens can be located. The cones which are produced and mature in one growing season, are distributed around the crown somewhat sporadically. Cones are generally only found on well established mature specimens which are well exposed to adequate sunlight and where there are sufficient trees for adequate pollination.

The cones are small and leathery, normally of six scales each carrying two winged seeds. These cones usually mature to shed their seed in the October/November period, and should be collected just prior to opening so that the seeds can be extracted after further drying and shaking.

It is reputed that occasional seed samples, or parts of them, exhibit embryo dormancy, however the greater proportion of seeds will germinate satisfactorily without exposure to a period of cold temperature. Nevertheless in common with many other conifers if the seeds are sown early and experience even a limited period of chilling, germination is not only enhanced but the rate of emergence is improved.

The seeds are relatively large for plants of the Thuja and Cypress group and losses in the seedbed are relatively few. The seeds are broadcast, firmed in and lightly covered to achieve a population of about 400 per square metre.

This species is not commonly grown from seed in the British nursery trade and reliable information on any particular aspects of production are scanty. Experience does confirm that late sown seed often emerges slowly and erratically while seed exposed to chilling normally germinates rapidly and effectively.

Seedlings normally achieve 10-15 cm height grade in the first year.

CARPINUS

The 'Hornbeam' *(Carpinus betulus)* is used extensively in the British Isles as an ornamental hedging plant, it also occurs frequently on suitable soil types as a native tree and is occasionally planted as a specimen in its own right, although for this purpose it is more often encountered in the fastigiate form. A number of alien species are cultivated but none is commonly encountered and their seed production in the U.K. is usually negligible, this latter factor largely being due to the unsuitability of climatic conditions at pollination and fertilisation.

Mature Hornbeam trees usually produce fruit in considerable quantities and as it is a reasonably common tree at least in the Southern Counties and Midlands, the local collection of seed should not present any problem.

A survey of the literature implies that the Hornbeam is erratic in its seedbearing habits, producing good crops of sound viable seed every two to four years. Experience in the South East and East Midlands however, has shown that consistent crops are produced almost annually and that failure in a particular year is usually due to uncharacteristic climatic conditions at a crucial stage in flower or fruit development. This is confirmed by observations that sheltered branches of seed bearing trees produce sound seed while fruits on the exposed branches are void.

If seed cannot be obtained locally it can readily be obtained from the commercial seedhouses either as cleaned seed or with the wings still attached. Of the alien species only *C. caroliniana* is regularly available, usually from North American sources.

Because crops of Hornbeam seed can usually be collected annually the necessity for storage on the nursery is not of great significance. If it is necessary to store seed it is usually stored dry and at a cool temperature, however, if the seed was properly clean of chaff it could be cold (1-3°C) stored at high humidity.

Seed is conventionally collected from the trees when it is mature i.e. just prior to dispersal (when the wings are brown and dry) and at this stage it will be found that the seed has developed a hard seedcoat and cold temperature type embryo dormancy controls. In such a condition the seed will need to be 91 stratified throughout the summer and the following winter before germination will occur. Seed purchased from a seedhouse will have been dried and will certainly be in this condition and so require the same treatment.

The hard seedcoat dormancy control develops as the fruit matures and dries out just prior to dispersal, if this condition could be avoided, then autumn sowing with consequent exposure to the winter's cold would allow germination in the following spring. When the seed is collected 'green' the hard seedcoat condition has not developed. However, it must not be collected before the embryo has matured and a sufficient food supply has been established if successful germination and seedling development is to be ensured. The most satisfactory stage for collection then, is as the wings reach a yellowish colour and are still pliable, drying out and hard seedcoat development at this stage will not have reached any significant proportions. If the fruits are collected during this period the seeds are best treated by immediate extraction from the wings and sowing on an open ground seedbed so that they are continually maintained in moist surroundings.

The seed should be separated from most of the wings in order to facilitate an accurate and even distribution at sowing. Dried fruits are easily dealt with by threshing and blowing away the chaff but immature fruits with soft wings present problems and there is no real alternative to hand work if separation is to be achieved adequately.

The seeds are broadcast sown onto the prepared seedbed, are lightly rolled in and then covered with grit. This type of autumn sowing should provide adequate chilling over the winter period for germination to occur in the spring. Hornbeam tends to be fairly late to germinate and emerge in the spring and it is, in consequence, less likely to be damaged by cold temperature; it will however be subject to damage by late season radiation frost unless adequate precautions are taken. Because of this late emergence, stratified seed can reasonably safely be spring sown without the danger of the seed being chitted.

More accurate and reliable stands of seedlings will be obtained by early collection and avoidance of the hard seedcoat condition. The rate at which seeds are sown will possibly depend on the subsequent use of the seedlings although it would appear practical to obtain the greatest productivity from the seedbed whatever is the subsequent use. Seedlings of a 35 to 45 cm grade with single sturdy stems will be produced at a population of approaching 300 per square metre. This may not be a sufficient population in the production of hedging plants: however if the density is increased individual size declines as would be expected.

CASTANEA

The 'Sweet Chestnut' *(Castanea sativa)* is an introduced tree which has 'gone native' very effectively and is widely naturalised in the southern part of the country. It makes a fine specimen tree in its own right or it can be grown as a rootstock for its own varieties and alien species. Occasionally it is still planted for coppicing.

As a species it is very variable in the quality of nuts which it produces; in the best types, i.e. those suitable for eating or as seeds, only one, or possibly sometimes two, nuts in each burr develop, in the remainder all four nuts develop and none becomes useful for seed purposes.

The seed is a typical 'nut' seed which deteriorates and loses viability rapidly with drying. Storage in a sealed polythene bag at 1°C to 3°C will prolong survival for up to twelve months. Unless special arrangements are made with the supplier, imported seed usually arrives after a period of dry storage and viability is declining. This can be arrested by soaking in water for twenty-four hours to reconstitute the seed or by mixing the seed with damp peat. On a large scale, cool storage in a suitably sited bin mixed with damp peat is probably the easiest nursery practice.

The performance of collected seed should be well over ninety per cent while that of imported seed will vary according to the degree and length of drying; at worst the seed is dead.

In order to prevent any loss in viability, collected seed should be autumn sown, if this is not possible cool moist storage to prevent drying is essential. Successful storage of seed can be recognised by the maintenance of the shiny, waxy seed coat, while deterioration is indicated by the development of a dull and ultimately wrinkled seedcoat.

The seed is large and can be station sown, it is sown to its own depth to achieve a population of 250 to 300 per square metre and, although not strictly necessary, it is covered with grit which facilitates water penetration and weeding. This density should provide one year old seedlings 40 to 60 cm tall and in the 8 to 12 mm grade. It is important that the seedlings are lifted as 1 + 0 in order to break the tap root and so ease transplanting and survival.

The seed is often infested with a curculionid weevil (*Balaninus sp*) the larvae of which burrows into the seed killing the embryo. Infested nuts can be discarded by floating in water and by visual observation at sowing. On a large scale warm water treatment of the seed (30 minutes at 40°C) is also practised.

Imported seed is often developing surface moulds of the Powdery Mildew type and these *may* well produce losses at germination. Fungicidal dusting will normally eliminate the problem, but it may be that ultimately this is not a useful practice if these fungi are associated with mycorchizal development.

Sound seed is extremely variable in size, depending variously on the ability of the tree to produce good nuts, its location and the quality of the summer. Seed from southern European sources is usually large and weighs approximately 100-120 per kilogram, whereas home produced seed (which may possibly produce hardier seedlings) is smaller, but perfectly acceptable, and weighs 140-200 per kilogram.

Although a hardy species, as one would expect of temperate region, woodland tree subjects, the very young seedlings are susceptible to damage from radiation frost when not protected by the forest canopy, however, as emergence is usually fairly late this may not be a problem.

Castanea appears to be fairly free from pests and diseases in the seed-bed, but should the mildew prove troublesome, dusting with captan or a suitable mercuric compound may then prove advantageous.

93

As seeds of this species are likely to be taken by rodents and birds at almost any season, it is advisable to dress them with a suitable repellent or taint them by mixing with paraffin.

CEDRUS

All the species of Cedar can be found as mature cone bearing trees in the British Isles, usually as single specimens or well spaced groups in the larger, well established, parks and gardens. They occur with reasonable frequency in the southern and western parts of the country but have not succeeded so well in the colder, drier north and east.

The female cones are fertilised in the early autumn and the seed bearing cones develop over the ensuing two growing seasons or just exceptionally in one. The seeds are dispersed by the scales of the cone breaking away from the central axis while still attached to the branch. Cones should be collected just prior to this stage so that they can be readily broken up and the seeds extracted.

The selection of parent trees to provide a source of seed requires some experience, observation and evaluation; as cone bearing trees do not invariably produce sound seed. The reasons for failure to set seed are not easily identifiable as cone and seed development are completely normal except for the development of the embryo and stored food. Failure may be due to continued vegetative growth of sufficient magnitude to prevent seed production, or possibly may be due to the necessity for cross pollination, or alternatively it may simply be a naturally periodic effect which is complicated by the vagaries of an alien climate during a lengthy period of cone maturation. Often the resultant 'seeds' under these conditions contains no embryo and are filled with an oily liquid.

Seed is readily obtainable from the normal commercial sources and provided the sample is from the current season's crop it will exhibit an adequate level of quality although some very poor samples are also encountered. Although there is no direct evidence suggesting that hardier races of Cedars do exist, it is very possible that such do occur and if attention is paid to their natural geographic range, to be expected. It would therefore be prudent to obtain seed collected from natural stands at high elevations rather than from cultivated trees in southern Europe. Observations have indicated however that the hardiness of individuals in any sample tends to be very variable.

The seed is soft and oily and deteriorates quickly on drying, it should not therefore be extracted from cones by dry heat. Commercial seed is chiefly collected in southern Europe and will almost inevitably be dried to some degree, however quality is acceptable and can be maintained at adequate levels by sealing in polythene bags and storing at between 1 and 3°C. This will provide short term storage for about twelve months. If collecting local seed it may prove to be more successful if the cones are collected intact and stored dry so that the seed can be extracted just prior to sowing, such a technique appears to preserve viability at very high levels in the short term (over winter).

94   Extraction from cones which do not disintegrate readily is said to be

achieved by soaking in warm water which causes the cone scales to open. If this is not successful Heit recommends freezing after soaking.

The seeds of *C. atlantica* and *C. libani* are much 'softer' than those of *C. deodara* and deteriorate much more quickly unless storage conditions are cool and moist.

Under normal circumstances none of the species exhibits any dormancy condition and germination will occur as soon as suitable environmental conditions are provided. American experience suggests that an improved germination response will be obtained with a small pre-chilling treatment. However, the viability of a sample can be assessed by an ordinary germination test. A normal level of viability is difficult to pronounce as commercial seed has always a diminished level because of extraction techniques and/or storage conditions between dispersal and despatch.

The seed is sown ideally on a seedbed with a high leaf litter (preferably coniferous) content so that conditions for the development of a satisfactory root system are enhanced.

As the seed does not exhibit any deep dormancy controls it should not be sown before March if the danger of exposure to radiation frost is to be avoided. It is sown broadcast on the finely prepared seedbed and pressed in to ensure sufficient water uptake.

A population of 500 seedlings per square metre provides a reasonable compromise between yield and individual seedling size for *C. deodara*; however this figure may be increased by as much as twenty per cent for *C. libani* and *C. atlantica*. The seedlings of the Deodar are more vigorous and at this density develop a complete cover by the end of the season.

C. deodara produces the biggest seeds and in general exhibits the best germination response and vigour of growth, for this reason it has gained favour as the rootstock for all the varieties of Cedars and especially those of *C. atlantica*.

The seedlings of all species of *Cedrus* are prone to 'Damping Off' just after emergence and as such an infection is likely to benefit from low temperatures and marginal frost damage it is advantageous to delay sowing for this reason as well.

Species	Seeds/kg	Pop./m^2	Seedling height
C. atlantica	$14,000 \pm 4,000$	750/800	± 15 cm
C. deodara	$8,000 \pm 2,000$	500	± 18 cm
C. libani	$13,000 \pm 4,000$	750/800	± 15 cm

ASSOCIATED READING

Heit, C.E. (1968) 'Propagation from Seed, 16. Testing and growing Cedrus species', Amer. Nurs. *128* (6) : 12.

CERCIS

This genus of leguminous shrubs and trees is usually represented in cultivation in the British Isles by the 'Judas Tree', *C. siliquastrum*, although the two 'Redbuds', *C. canadensis* and *C. chinensis* are occasionally available.

The Judas Tree flowers early in the season and once established its flower production is profuse, the season for seed and fruit development is consequently long and good and regular crops of seeds are produced, at least in the South of England. Neither *C. canadensis* nor *C. chinensis* have been observed to set seed in the climate encountered in Britain although no doubt they do in exceptional seasons.

The fruits of the Judas Tree are typical leguminous pods containing up to twelve seeds. These must be collected before they shed their seeds, dried and then flailed to extract the seeds. Seeds of other species must necessarily be imported from commercial sources. If freshly collected seed is available and it is sown directly during the autumn then germination of the complete sample will occur in the spring. Seed from seedhouses will inevitably have experienced some drying and if sown on receipt will usually show partial germination in the ensuing spring, the remaining portion will have developed a sufficiently hard seedcoat to delay germination until the second spring. Lengthy periods of dry storage will enhance the hardness of the seedcoat and suitable treatment to overcome this condition will be necessary if germination is to be regulated. The treatment required will depend, on the degree to which the hard seedcoat has developed, normally a warm water treatment is sufficient but should the condition prove intractable sulphuric acid digestion will be required.

C. siliquastrum alba will produce a proportion of its seedling population true to name, especially if the parent plants are grown as a single stand group. It would seem feasible to rogue the seedbed for normal pink flowered plants as the albino form has a paler leaf and lacks colour in the leafstalk.

The literature suggests that at least some samples of the Eastern Redbud (*C. canadensis*) possess embryo dormancy and that early sowing to allow for a period of chilling would prove beneficial, after the seedcoat condition has been countered. Experience suggests that *C. siliquastrum* does not exhibit embryo dormancy as germination can be achieved quite satisfactorily by sowing under glass without exposure to chilling.

The seeds are sown normally on a prepared seedbed and covered in the conventional fashion to achieve a population of about 250 seedlings per square metre.

Seedlings of *Cercis* should be lifted and containerised at the end of the first season, as plants of older vintage grown in the open ground are not notoriously difficult to re-establish.

Reference to a selection of commercial seedhouse catalogues indicates that the following species and varieties are usually available.

Species	Seedcount ,000s/kg
C. canadensis	38.0
C. chinensis	46.0
C. occidentalis	+
C. siliquastrum	45.0
C. siliquastrum alba	45.0

ASSOCIATED READING

McDaniel, J.C. (1971) 'White flowered *Cercis canadensis* from seed', The plant Prop. *17* (1) : 21.
Robertson, K.H. (1976), '*Cercis* — The Redbuds', Arnoldia *36* (2) : 37.

CHAMAECYPARIS

Although there are six or so species of 'False Cypresses' only two are likely to be produced from seed in nursery practice — *C. lawsoniana*, both as a hedging plant and as a rootstock and *C. nootkatensis* occasionally for growing as a specimen in its own right.

Both species fruit prolifically in the British Isles producing their typical, spherical small cones which mature in the late summer to autumn period of the year in which they are pollinated. The cones open slowly on the tree to liberate the seeds so that effective collection is achieved by collecting the fruits as they mature and then drying them artificially at around 30°C, under these conditions the cone scales open quickly and the seeds can be readily shaken free. Usually the yield is about 20 to 30 seeds per cone.

In common with other subjects which produce masses of seed (viz. *Betula*, *Liriodendron* and *Salix)* the quality is usually poor and germination rates even from vigorous crops is relatively light.

Seeds of these species will usually germinate *in toto* without previous chilling although a short period of chilling by exposure to cold in the seedbed will normally enhance both the rate of germination and the uniformity of emergence.

Samples of Lawson Cypress seed can be obtained from single stands of particular cultivars, and will produce a fair proportion of similar offspring in the seedling population but these have little value other than to produce particular seedling variants for hedging purposes, nowadays vegetatively propagated plants for this purpose are not appreciably more expensive.

Early spring sowing therefore produces a reasonable crop emergence and few problems are normally encountered: as might be anticipated the seedlings are not frost hardy and will require conventional protection. If the season, in the early stages, is cold and damp patchy losses due to various damping off conditions may occur, but routine preventive measures should mitigate against any outbreak.

Species	Seedcount ,00s/kg
C. lawsoniana	c 400
C. nootkatensis	c 250 $\pm$ 15%

CLEMATIS

This large family of both climbing and herbaceous subjects is widely grown and the various species show a tremendous range through the temperate regions of the northern hemisphere. It is more normal for all Clematis to be propagated vegetatively nowadays and this is conventionally achieved by various types of stem cuttings. However Clematis have traditionally been propagated by grafting and even today this system is used for the production of flowering plants of the large flowered hybrids in one season and the propagation of the more intractable species by stem cutting (such as *C. armandii*). Certain species are also propagated from seed to be grown in their own right viz. *C. tangutica* and *C. orientalis*.

However the chief reason for seedling production of Clematis is in the production of rootstocks; and the system adopted is aimed at producing a particular quality regarded as suitable for this purpose. The aim being usually to produce seedlings with a hypocotyl diameter of 2.5 mm although some propagators prefer bigger seedlings and graft onto any suitably sized roots.

Seed of any species required for open seedbed production can normally be produced in the British Isles and even a relatively small stock plant will usually produce much seed. However viability is often low in some of the alien species. *C. vitalba,* the native 'Traveller's Joy' or 'Old Man's Beard' and *C. viticella* are usually grown for rootstocks and both produce good seed, as indeed does *C. tangutica.*

The main problem in dealing with the seed is separating the fruits because of the long and feathery tail which causes them to adhere together — drying and threshing so that the tails are broken up, helps to alleviate the problem although the mixture must be sown as it is not easy to separate the seed from the trash without specialised equipment.

Clematis is reputed to exhibit dormancy controls of the cold temperature type but as the seeds can be readily germinated in a warm glasshouse it would appear that chilling is unnecessary; but this condition well may bear some relationship to time of collection, and as the seeds remain on the plant until well into the late winter it is possible that they could be chilled on the parent and that the chilling requirement is small. However it would be as well to sow as early as possible, as exposure to cold appears to enhance both emergence and rate of germination, at least in the open ground situation.

No special seedbed requirements are apparent and the seed should be sown to achieve a population depending on the quality of the seedbed, of between 400 and 600 per square metre.

The counts of seed lots of *Clematis* species vary dramatically depending on the degree of drying, the cleanness of the sample — i.e. how much trash has been removed, and the proportion of void fruits.

Species	Seedcount in ,000s/kg	Fruits ,000s/kg
C. tangutica	350	x
C. vitalba	700	c. 100
C. viticella	505	x

CORNUS

The genus *Cornus* is a variable group of shurbs and rarely trees which are distributed sporadically throughout the north temperate regions of the world. They are mostly deciduous and the greater portion can be readily propagated vegetatively; so that propagation from seed is limited to the production of:—

(a) those species required in large numbers for natural cover plantings or hedges,
(b) rootstocks for working with selected varieties and
(c) specimen plants in their own right.

The following species represent the normal range:—

C. alba	—	for cover and hedging
C. controversa	—	as specimens
C. florida	—	for rootstocks and specimens
C. kousa	—	as specimens
C. nutallii	—	as specimens
C. sanguinea	—	for cover and hedging

Dormancy conditions in some species delay germination until the second spring after dispersal due to the development of a hard seedcoat but otherwise a conventional cold temperature type dormancy is the usual pattern.

In general the tree species are biennial in their production of seed crops while the shrubby dogwoods produce quite adequate crops in most years.

The fruit of the dogwood is a fleshy berry containing one large nutlet type, stone which is nominally two seeded. The flesh of these drupaceous fruits is active in enhancing dormancy of the seed as it ripens and it is therefore important that fruits should be collected as soon as they change colour and separated from the flesh directly. Seeds of *C. florida, C. alba,* and *C. sanguinea* under natural conditions only exhibit embryo dormancy so that autumn sowing or a winters stratification is sufficient to allow germination in the spring.

Imported seed of *C. mas, C. nuttallii* and *C. kousa* have developed hard seedcoats in storage. *C. mas* can be collected in all but very dull years in the United Kingdom but invariably it produces a hard seedcoat if left to maturity, the only way to avoid the problem has been the collection of 'green' fruits; apparently this has worked satisfactorily and with such an early flowering subject, it should prove a relatively easy to determine the correct 'green' stage, the limited evidence available suggests that this might be as early as July.

The hard coat of the stone can be digested with sulphuric acid or can be reduced by mechanical scarification if germination is required in the first spring after collection otherwise the seedcoat can be reduced by a warm summer's stratification.

All the available sources of information emphasise the importance of collecting, extracting and sowing fresh seed for maximum germination the following spring and the early collection of those subjects producing hard seedcoats. However, this is very much limited by the species which will produce seed in the British Isles.

The seeds should be broadcast sown on a conventional, well manured seedbed to achieve a population of about 350 seedlings per square metre. Germination is normally early in the spring, especially with early sown, fresh seed samples; dried samples may be delayed if a marginal hard seedcoat condition has developed. Protection for early emerging seedlings will therefore be needed if damage from late spring radiation frosts is to be avoided.

The seedlings do not appear to be susceptible to particular problems in the seedbed.

Species	Count of cleaned stones ,000s/kg	No, of seeds %
C. alba	30.0	+25
C. sanguinea	20.0	+20
C. kousa	18.0	
C. florida	10.0	+10
C. mas	6.0	
C. nutallii	11.0	

The problem with the various Cornus is determining the proportions of double seeded stones, single seeded stones and void stones so that an estimate of the number of seeds per unit weight of stones can be assessed.

CORYLUS

The 'Hazel' *(Corylus avellana)* is a well known wayside and hedge plant in most of southern England. The 'Filbert' *(C. maxima)* is of course grown as a nut crop in the South East together with the Hazel and Cob nut, but apart from these two subjects no other species are at all commonly cultivated in Great Britain although several other species are successful and ornamental.

The various fruiting forms and decorative varieties are propagated vegetatively and this is still generally achieved by grafting onto a rootstock. Hence seedling rootstocks will be required.

The genus is a relatively small one and from an ornamental point of view the numbers in cultivation can be reduced because several species may be very similar, differing only in their geographical distribution viz. *C. colurna* from Western Asia *C. chinensis* from Central Asia and *C. jacquemontii* from the Himalaya.

The various species are most satisfactorily produced from seed and although mature seed bearing plants can be located, fruit production in the alien species is often variable in the British climate. However supplies of a good range can fairly readily be obtained from commercial sources, these will inevitably have been subject to drying but in the short term this has only a marginal influence on viability.

Seed can be collected when it is ripe and dispersed, by picking up from the ground but under normal circumstances such an opportunity will be pre-empted by squirrels and various rodents. Seed should therefore be picked as it begins to ripen, but subsequent treatment must involve some drying in order to enable the separation of the husks from the seed. Soundness of the seed is normally good although some may be infested with weevils which eat the entire content of the nut. These can easily be separated by flotation.

Corylus seeds can be stored relatively easily for two to three years by keeping in a sealed container at 3 to 4°C.

Seeds of *C. avellana* have been shown to possess no embryo dormancy at dispersal but that further drying (as will occur in storage) induces inhibitor development and a consequent chilling requirement before germination will occur.

Seeds of most species will show some germination if spring sown but most samples of dried imported seed have developed fairly marked embryo dormancy and require a reasonably substantial period of chilling if uniform and rapid germination is to be achieved.

This can best be achieved by autumn sowing as soon as the fruits have been collected, cleaned and sorted. Imported seed which arrives later should be well mixed with plenty of damp peat and stored at 1 to 3°C for at least 12 to 14 weeks before spring sowing.

The seed should be broadcast sown to produce a seedling density of between 200 to 250 per square metre, if the seed has been reasonably sorted and the sample is sound few losses should be anticipated. The seed is large enought to handle and can be station sown, or drilled if required.

The seedbed should be lightly prepared so that the seeds can readily be rolled or pressed in for best contact and water uptake. The surface is then covered with grit in order to maintain good aeration.

Hazel seedlings do not normally suffer from particular pests or diseases and provided husbandry is adequate, a good quality crop in the 30 to 40 cm grade can be expected. Normally only the following species are grown as seedlings:—

C. avellana   — for rootstock or hedging
C. colurna   — as a small tree
C. sieboldiana — as an ornamental shrub.

In addition the following species are usually available from commercial seed sources:—

C. americana   (like *C. avellana*)
C. chinensis   (like *C. colurna*)
C. cornuta   (like *C. sieboldiana*)
C. maxima
C. heterophylla (like *C. avellana*)

C. cornuta appears to develop a hard seedcoat and does not naturally germinate until the second spring after dispersal. Seed size, in nut seeds of this type, is usually very variable both from source to source and year to year. In a normal year a good source of *C. avellana* in southern England will yield about 750 seeds per kg.

COTONEASTER

The genus *Cotoneaster* is a medium sized but diverse group of woody plants   101 which vary from small, very prostrate ground cover subjects to fairly large, long lived plants the size of small trees. The greater proportion of cotoneasters, grown in the nursery trade, are hybrid in origin or are particular selected clones of the various species and for these types vegetative propagation is an essential. The usual systems of vegetative propagation involved are by cuttings — usually for the small leaved subjects and by grafting onto a rootstock for the larger growing forms. Large numbers of a limited range of species however are produced from seed for the following purposes:—

(a) for use as ground cover plantings etc. e.g. *C. horizontalis,*
(b) for use in a semi wild situation as wild life and game food sources e.g. *C. bullatus, C. salicifolius.*
(c) as rootstocks e.g. *C. bullatus, C. frigidus.*
(d) for hedging plants e.g. *C. lacteus, C. simonsii.*

The chief problem associated with the seedling production of cotoneasters is the obtaining of reliable true-to-name seed. The species of this genus are notoriously promiscuous and hybrid seed is readily produced if suitable species for cross pollination are adjacent. Seed material should therefore be collected either in the wild from single species stands or should be obtained in cultivation from a group of the same species which are themselves reliably true to name, for although cultivated plants may appear to possess the correct qualities it is important that they should be genetically correct and produce a uniform batch of reliable seedlings.

A number of Cotoneaster species are of course, apomictic and seed can be collected from these with confidence, even though they may be adjacent to and in close proximity to other species. The fruits of Cotoneasters are very similar to those of Crataegus and Sorbus in form, and contain similar nutlets although in structure and appearance they are not dissimilar to the achenes of *Rosa.*

The seed is extracted from the fruit by maceration and flotation, in this way the broken pulp and any void or unsound seeds is removed. This method of extraction provides a sound seed sample so that a good germination response is obtained.

The fruits are relatively small pomes containing usually up to five seeds and these mature in the late autumn. Crops from year to year vary both in quality of seed production and in the degree to which the seeds are infested by the grubs of chalcid type insects.

The majority of species produce seeds which develop a hard seedcoat condition which causes the delay of germination for a year. The seeds must perforce receive a season of warm stratification to reduce the seedcoat prior to chilling although sulphuric acid digestion is feasible and has been used commercially. There does not appear to be any direct evidence to suggest that the collection of 'green' berries and the extraction of seeds at this stage will avoid the hard seedcoat condition although it is reasonable to expect that it will. There are occasional references in the literature, albeit vaguely, to improve germination being obtained from fruits collected well before they are ripe.

Because of the hard seededness Cotoneasters can safely be stored dry under cool conditions for two to three years without undue loss of viability.

The seed should be sown broadcast to achieve a population of about 350 per square metre. Autumn to winter sowing will provide an adequate period of chilling before germination will occur.

Seedling cotoneasters do not appear to be susceptible to any particular pests and diseases in the seedbed which require any special precautions.

ASSOCIATED READING

Giersbach, J. (1934), 'After ripening and germination of Cotoneaster seeds', Contrib. Boyce Thompson Inst. *6* (3):323.

CRATAEGUS

Ideally it would be desirable to raise all thorn species from seed but because of the problems in obtaining reliable seed from a pure stand source and because of their considerable within species variation and proneness to hybridise, it is basically an impractical proposition. In addition the propagator has to deal with the problems associated with the stratification of the, individually, small quantities involved and the sowing of each batch of seed separately; this makes it unacceptable as a commercial practice. Hence these subjects are produced, in present day nursery practice, by working virtually all this genus onto an easily produced and readily available rootstock.

Most authors, when describing techniques of propagation for the ornamental thorns accept the prevalent commercial practice of working all the genus onto rootstocks of the european "White Thorn" or "Hawthorn" *(C. monogyna)* and indeed those trees which do develop are of adequate size and proportions. However in current nursery practice many of the species and varieties show some degree of compatibility variation down the nursery row. The north american species, especially, exhibit markedly high levels of incompatibility when worked on rootstocks of the european Hawthorns. This overall total of failures which, for one reason or another, do not make a saleable tree in the crop often reaches unacceptably high levels.

The two european Thorns native to the British Isles, which are usually available for rootstock purposes, are *C. monogyna,* and *C. oxyacantha.* The majority of seedlings offered for this purpose are selected from the vast numbers which are produced annually as hedging plants. Those plants of a suitable grade with a single straight stem are selected out and sold as rootstocks. However problems arise because of the uncertainity of the identity of these rootstocks, they may be all of one species or the other, but usually are a mixture of both, and it is this factor which appears to enhance the compatibility problems. If the rootstocks are just one species then the incompatibility which becomes apparent will be due to the inherent variation within that species when worked with a particular scion variety. However, a mixture produces a variation which is attributable to the differential variations between two species in relation to any particular scion variety. It would therefore be prudent to obtain or produce these two subjects separately so that such problems could be reduced to an acceptable minimum in the nursery and use *C. oxyacantha* as a rootstock for its own varieties and *C. monogyna* similarly.

103

As the north american species often exhibit particularly poor levels of compatibility and vigour of growth when worked on either of these european thorns it would be wise to produce seedling rootstocks of a species from this geographic group. The most suitable tree for this purpose in terms of vigour, broad spectrum compatibility and availability of seed would appear to be the 'Cockspur Thorn' *(C. crus galli)*. Extracted seed or dried berries of this species are available in most years from the wholesale seedhouses. Berries can be collected from mature fruiting specimens locally although there seems to be some doubt concerning the exact taxonomic position of the vegetatively propagated clone which is distributed under this name in the United Kingdom, however, this does not preclude its use as a rootstock as the seedlings have proved to be acceptably uniform.

In order therefore to provide an adequate selection of rootstocks for the diversity and number of species grown, but attempting to rationalise these in terms of total number grown, requires the production of an identifiable range of rootstocks for this genus so that incompatibility problems can be reduced to a minimum. In this respect *C. monogyna* and/or *C. oxyacantha* should be used for the european (i.e. cut leaf) types and *C. crus-galli* or *C. coccinea* for the american (i.e. entire leaf) subjects.

The fruit of the thorn, generally termed a 'Haw' is a pome enclosing a number of seeds which are generally hard coated nutlets. The haw will usually contain the same number of seeds as the number of styles within the flower although if this exceeds five some seeds in each fruit fail to develop or abort and it is therefore wise to sample each parent tree to ascertain the average number of seeds in each fruit each year.

The seeds (i.e. the nutlets) of virtually all Hawthorns have a hard seedcoat and in the majority of species this is impermeable and so requires the normal decomposing activity of one season to reduce it to the level at which it will not prevent imbibition. The embryo then requires exposure to a period of cold temperature to break dormancy. Thorns are very typical of the *Rosaceae* in terms of dormancy, and although it would be quite feasible to extract from the flesh, reduce with sulphuric acid and either sow directly or cold temperature treat artificially, they are normally stratified as this technique produces an acceptable proportion of germinable seeds. The remaining species, although they have a 'hard' seedcoat, will imbibe directly and merely require a period of chilling.

Species exhibiting the hard seedcoat condition and requiring a period of chilling to overcome embryo dormancy:—

> *C. crus-galli* L.
> *C. flava* Ait.
> *C. monogyna* Jacq.
> *C. oxyacantha* L.
> *C. prunifolia* (Poir.) Pers.
> *C. punctata* Jacq.
> *C. rotundifolia* Moench.

Species requiring a period of chilling to overcome embryo dormancy only:—

> *C. coccinea* L.
> *C. mollis* Scheele
> *C. cordata* Ait.

Periods of dry storage appear to enhance the hard seedcoat effect in this latter group, if therefore seed of these species is bought in, it may be worth checking their ability to imbibe and if they do not, stratify them over the summer as for the first group. However often the seeds of this latter group, after commercial processing, are of poor quality and viability is low, which together with low initial viability at harvest may cause the low level of imbibition.

The fruits are collected relatively early in the season while the flesh is still 'unripe' so that any possibility of inhibitors being produced by the flesh and permeating the seed is reduced to a minimum. The seeds are extracted by maceration and floatation. So that dormancy development will be limited, the seeds should be immediately stratified to prevent further hardening of the seedcoat.

If stratifying clean seed in sand or grit it would be advantageous to use a grade which can readily be screened out prior to sowing so that a count and a viability test can be made.

The stratified seed is sown broadcast onto the seedbed, rolled in and covered with grit. This operation should be carried out in the late autumn — early winter period as Thorn seed is very prone to early chitting and considerable losses can be incurred if seed is sown in this condition.

In the seedbed Thorns are particularly susceptible to Mildew caused by *Podosphaera oxycanthae,* which produces the typical white powdering of the leaves and severely checks seedling growth. It is readily controlled by *routine* sprays of Benomyl or by sulphur based materials.

In assessing the population required to produce seedling Thorns it should be borne in mind that although an adequate height is required (50-60 cm) the seedlings are to be used as rootstocks, and therefore must have a straight, upright stem and a minimum number of lateral branches. This can only be achieved by planting sufficiently close together and a population of 400 per square metre will achieve this situation provided that continued attention is paid to feeding and Mildew control.

Because of tap root development Thorn seedlings should not be kept in the seedbed for more than one year.

Species	Seeds/kg
Crataegus crus-galli	15,400
Crataegus monogyna	8,000
Crataegus oxyacantha	10,000
Crataegus coccinea	20,000

Seeds of most thorns are enclosed in a hard nutlet and in those species which produce several nutlets per fruit, especially, assessment should be made of viability as although the nutlets develop they are frequently empty. The viability of imported seed is often very low, however this may be a characteristic of the particular species (e.g. *C. coccinea*) although this lack of embryo may be well be due to infestation by insect larvae.

ASSOCIATED READING

Cumming, W.A. (1964) *'Crataegus* rootstock studies', Proc. Int. Plant. Prop. Soc., *14*: 146-149.

Flemion, F. (1938) 'Breaking the dormancy of seeds of *Crataegus* species,' Contrib. Boyce Thompson Inst. *9* (5):409.

CUPRESSUS

Three members of this genus — *C. arizonica, C. macrocarpa* and *C. torulosa* might occasionally be propagated from seed in this country. Of these only *C. macrocarpa* has any real relevance insofar as it is used as a windbreak or hedging plant in the milder areas and may be required as a rootstock for its yellow/golden varieties.

Remarks made for Chamaecyparis also apply to this genus with the proviso that these species are only marginally hardy as seedlings. Seed collection is also less urgent as the cones often take several years to open while still attached to the tree.

Species	Seedcount ,000s/kg.
C. macrocarpa	c.145

CYTISUS

These types of 'Brooms' are usually propagated by vegetative means for two main reasons — i) the majority of subjects grown are hybrids or varieties and require vegetative methods and ii) as these subjects are almost invariably pot grown, propagation from stem cuttings fits the production system more satisfactorily.

However a few species, and especially *C. scoparius* are required in very large plantings for motorway work, reclamation and conservation and are necessarily propagated from seed to cope with the scale of operation. *Cytisus sp.* are more prone to develop intractable hard seedcoats than their close relatives, the genus *Genista,* and these can be difficult if old or dried seed only is available. Seed of the current season, collected and extracted and sown straight away germinates well in the following spring as there is sufficient warm season left to reduce the seedcoat.

The seeds of this genus are dispersed by explosion of the pod and it is important to collect prior to this stage.

Species	Seedcount in ,000s/kg
C. albus	275
C. nigricans	230
C. purpureus	125
C. scoparius	120

C. battandierii is also readily propagated from seed but as it is rarely produced in large quantities it is normally germinated under glass.

DAPHNE

The various species of Daphne tend to be propagated vegetatively in nursery practice as the range of variation, especially in flower characteristics, is wide and in consequence desirable clonal selections have occurred. Few Daphnes either are grown on a sufficient scale to warrant the large outdoor seedling production considered here, however all species can be readily propagated from seed if it is available, and all would seem to respond broadly to the same system.

Many of the rarer sorts of Daphnes, which cannot readily be propagated from cuttings, are produced by grafting onto rootstocks, *D. laureola* or *D. mezereum* are commonly produced from seed, the former as a woodland garden subject or for game feed plantings and the latter as an early flowering decorative shrub. As the variants of these two types, which are commonly encountered in cultivation, also occur in the wild it is possible by suitable progeny testing and selection of the mother plant to obtain seedling populations which come true to type; and this is relatively simple if a pure stand group is established as a seed source. The varieties *alba*, *grandiflora* and 'Rubra' of *D. mezereum* and *D. laureola phillipii* all respond well to this husbandry. In some early dutch work van der Graaf has shown that the more vigorous plants of *D. mezereum* produce paler flowers in general and that is therefore necessary to progeny test all proposed mother plants as pale coloured flowers usually dominate in the next generation. Ir. B.C.M. van Elk of Proefstation voor de Boomkwederij te Boskoop writes 'At the Research Station a lot of work has been done on these selections and up until 1970 seedlings have been distributed each year as *Daphne mezereum* 'Rubra select'. One grower in the Boskoop area has also selected a more or less variable type called Daphne mezereum 'Ruby Glow'.

The species and forms of major commercial importance fruit abundantly in the British Isles and it has been suggested that this habit may have some bearing on the relatively short lived condition these species usually exhibit: although this factor is probably more attributable to the presence of a virus disease of ubiquitous distribution and which causes a typical chlorotic mottling of the leaves in *D. mezereum*. Fortunately this disease does not appear to be seed transmitted.

The seeds of *Daphne* are borne in single seeded berries which are particularly sought after by birds (especially blackbirds) as soon as they ripen and should be harvested quickly at this stage to avoid losing the crop.

Commercial seed is usually available as dried berries and in this condition will normally show a delay in germination until the second season after dispersal. Cleaned and dried seed will also respond similarly. In nature the seed will often germinate normally because passage through the bird's digestive tract reduces the seedcoat to a level at which imbibition will occur: drying, under commercial collection techniques, merely enhances this hard seedcoat condition.

The seeds of *Daphne* present a problem not only in developing a hard seedcoat condition but they require subsequently, after imbibition, a period of chilling before germination will occur. This hard seedcoat effect can be overcome either by a period of warm stratification or more satisfactorily by sulphuric acid digestion, although treatment time for this   107 latter technique will vary according to whether the cleaned seed or dried berries are used. The other alternative is to maintain a tame blackbird!

It is quite feasible with the fruits of this genus however to collect the berries in a 'green' condition, extract the seeds and sow immediately so that germination will occur in the following spring and the dormancy problem is avoided. Over thirty years ago a dutch trial was established to determine how soon green berries could be collected without detriment to the food store and embryo. Observations for *D. mezereum* showed that this could be done as early as the latter part of June.

The seeds should be sown to produce a population of about 350 per square metre and if necessary could be left in the seedbed for a second year as growth in the first year is not great.

ASSOCIATED READING

Amsler, A.M. (1953) 'Daphnes', J. Roy. Hort. Soc. *78*:5.
Anon. (1944) 'Kruising en zaadwinning van *Daphne mezereum* L.', Jaarb. Veren. 'De Proeftuin', Boskoop 1944:45.
Argles G.K. and P. Rowe-Dutton (1969) 'The propagation of daphnes', Nurs. Gard. Centre *148*:505.
Van der Graaf, A.J. (1945) 'Selectie van zaad planten van *Daphne mezereum* L.', Jaarb. Veren. 'De Proeftuin' Boskoop 1945.11. (1950) 'Daphne selectie', Jaarb. Veren. 'De Proeftuin' Boskoop (1950):75, (1951):70 and (1952):28.

DAVIDIA

This monotypic genus is constituted with the 'Dove Tree' or 'Pocket Handkerchief Tree' — *D. involucrata,* although there is a natural variant — *vilmoriniana* — with felted under surfaces to the leaves which sometimes is accorded specific rank.

There are many sizeable, mature fruiting trees to be found in parks and gardens throughout the country and the fruits can be readily collected either from the tree or the ground in the September-October period.

The fruit is oval to pear shaped and fleshy, about 4 cm. long; this contains a hard ridged nut containing from two to five seeds.

Production of seedlings of this plant is complicated by the hard fruit coat and the subsequent epicotyl dormancy exhibited by the embryo.

Initially the fruits should be warm stratified in order to allow decomposition of the hard seedcoat and the emergence of the radicle; subsequently a winter's chilling overcomes the epicotyl dormancy and the seedlings appear above the surface.

Practically this is achieved by placing the complete fruits in a box of damp peat and leaving them exposed to normal season temperatures. In the following autumn the seeds (with emerged radicle) can be separated and sown individually onto a conventional prepared seedbed. The chilling provided by the winter overcomes the inhibitions to shoot development and germination is completed in the spring.

The seedlings are relatively hardy for a chinese native in our variable climate but protection should be provided against radiation frosts.

No special problems are encountered in the seedbed — albeit from limited experience of outdoor growing.

FAGUS

The 'Common Beech' is one of the most stately and impressive of our native trees and although the genus does contain a number of other species, none is widely grown or offered in the nursery trade. The tree is grown virtually always from a seedling as vegetative propagation, other than by grafting onto a rootstock, has proved difficult and unreliable.

Seedlings are produced for the following uses:—
  (i) as hedging plants,
 (ii) for development as specimen standard trees,
(iii) as rootstocks.

The fruit of the Beech is a capsule which opens to release two seeds or 'nuts' which fall to the ground. Beech is the classic example of a subject exhibiting periodic seed production and is reputed to produce crops of 'mast' or seed only once in seven years, in fact the periodicity of production is more variable. Fortunately not all trees respond in the same cycle so that some supplies of seed can be collected in most years if sufficient stands of trees are observed. In the 'off' years crops of fruits are produced but the seeds contained in them are void.

Purple leaved Beech is always in short supply as a hedging plant but seed collected from parents with the same characteristic will usually produce a tolerably acceptable proportion of crop with coloured leaves, and provided the crop is rogued in the seedbed will produce a useful crop of purple leaved seedlings. If sufficient parent trees are available to progeny test then a high proportion of acceptable seedlings can be produced.

The seeds are collected by sweeping or picking up under the trees, these are then floated in water in order to separate the detritus and test the soundness of the seed. Weevils will infest the seed, eating out the embryo and foodstore.

Seed deteriorates rapidly with dry storage as would be expected in a subject which stores its food to some degree in lipid form and viability declines fairly quickly. After collection and sorting the seeds should not be held in bulk storage for too long as they tend to heat up and kill the embryo, unless the field heat is first removed and the crop is kept cool. Ideal storage consists of mixing with moist peat, to prevent drying, and holding at 3 to 4°C. On a large scale the nuts are stored in heaps mixed with damp peat and are turned at regular intervals, the object of the exercise being to keep the nuts plump and polished in appearance, which is a good external measure of the maintenance of good viability.

Provided that seedbed area is available, autumn sowing alleviates the storage problem and maintains the seed in good condition, unfortunately Beech nuts are sought after by many birds and rodents, especially squirrels and crows and precautions must be taken if the crop is not to be lost.

109

Beech nuts do not appear to have a chilling requirement before germination will occur but certainly germination is enhanced by exposure to cold prior to suitable conditions for germination.

The seeds are sown broadcast on a lightly prepared seedbed and then firmed in. The density of sowing can be varied quite significantly depending upon the use to which the seedlings are to be put although a crop of small seedlings may not even be very useful for hedging purposes. Seedlings of adequate size (35-50 cm) compatible with seedbed productivity will be produced at populations of 300 to 350 per square metre.

Beech seed is available from many commercial sources on the continent but if dry seed with low vitality is to be avoided then it is necessary to make special arrangements for delivery as soon as the crop is harvested. If seed is dry on receipt then it should be remoistened by mixing with damp peat as soon as is feasible. In the long term, local collection of seed is the most satisfactory and reliable system for ensuring a crop with high viability.

The seedcount for Beech is usually about 4,000+ per kg but fresh seed will weigh more heavily because of its higher water content.

ASSOCIATED READING

Anon. (1962) 'Collection and storage of acorns and beech mast', For. Comm. Lflt. *28*.
Buszewiez, B. (1962) 'Longevity of Beechnuts in relation to storage conditions', Rep. on For. Res. 1961 : 117.

FOTHERGILLA

This small genus of 'Bottle Brush Bushes' from the Witch Hazel family can be propagated from seed. However the author has no experience of these plants and can only refer the reader to the cited reference which will provide the most likely effective and reliable recommendations.

ASSOCIATED READING

Fordham, A.J. (1971) 'The propagation of Fothergilla', Arnoldia 31:256.

FRAXINUS

The Ashes are readily produced from seed and in those situations where seed is available from local sources or can be obtained from commercial seedhouses, this system of propagation is the most satisfactory method for producing a reliable crop. However, there are a number of variants and these must necessarily be produced vegetatively and at present they are normally propagated by working onto a field lined seedling rootstock.

The genus divides itself, in horticultural terms into two groups: those species described as the 'Flowering Ashes' typified by *F. ornus* and the 'Common Ash' of which *F. excelsior* is the best known example. In traditional nursery practice all Ashes have been worked onto rootstocks of *F.*

excelsior without undue detriment to the resulting tree, but it would be reasonable to produce rootstocks of say *F. ornus,* as a rootstock for the Flowering Ashes if only to produce a better relationship between scion and rootstock in terms of vigour.

The seeds of Ash are generally enclosed in a winged fruit (a samara) which is normally dispersed by wind. All species exhibit some form of dormancy control associated with germination of the seeds.

Some fifteen species are at all commonly encountered in cultivation in this country but only a few are sufficiently widely grown that seed is readily obtainable, however seed viability holds up well with dry storage and good samples of a fair range of species can be obtained from commercial sources.

Ash species do not appear to exhibit any regular patterns of periodicity in their seed production. The occasional years when a poor crop develops can usually be attributed to the occurrence of unusual or adverse climatic conditions at flowering or fruit set.

Traditionally seeds of this genus have been stored dry at room temperatures and under these conditions *F. excelsior* and some of the north american species maintain good levels of viability. The flowering Ashes, however, do not survive so well. Observations made in the United States have demonstrated that a greatly improved storage life is achieved if seeds are not dried and are stored at low temperatures. In nursery practice best results are achieved if the seed is collected before it is fully dried on the tree and is then stored at 1 to 3°C sealed in a polythene bag.

Under normal circumstances the fruits of *F. excelsior* remain on the tree until late winter or early spring and at this stage they have dried and are dispersed by wind. In this condition the seeds have an immature embryo, a hard seedcoat of short term effectiveness and after embryo maturation a requirement for cold temperature treatment. Stored seed (especially under dry warm conditions) also exhibits an enhanced hard seedcoat condition. The fruits therefore require immediate stratification in order to cause decomposition of the seedcoat, allow imbibition and subsequent embryo maturation during the summer months. After this the seed will need exposure to cold and this can be achieved in the seedbed by autumn sowing or by continued stratification until just after midwinter. The seed must be sown prior to chitting and regular checks are necessary to avoid running over into this state. Hence the production of Common Ash seedlings is a two season process unless artificial environments are available, however this problem can be avoided and the seed germinated in the first spring after dispersal if the seed is collected during the previous late summer while the fruits are still 'green'. At this stage the seed has not developed hard seedcoat, there is little further imbibition required by the seed and warm temperature for embryo maturation can be provided in the seedbed by immediate sowing: the seed is then subjected to chilling overwinter in the seedbed and germination occurs in the spring.

The Flowering Ashes do not exhibit such complex dormancy problems and if collected and sown in the late autumn or winter will germinate in the following spring. Some north american species *viz. F. americana* and *F. pensylvanica* also respond similarly.

F. excelsior is normally grown for rootstock use in the nursery trade and 111 there is now evidence to suggest that it is necessary to select parent trees. Dutch work, which has as yet been unconfirmed in the United Kingdom, suggests that in a population of rootstocks there is colour variation in the growing tip and that those which develop a purple colouration of the young leaves and bark exhibit marked incompatibility with normal scion varieties. It is therefore necessary to progeny test parent trees and selected fruits only from those which produce green seedlings: alternately the seedbed must be rogued rigorously.

The seed should be sown broadcast onto a normal seedbed to achieve a population of about 350 seedlings per square metre. A seedbed with a good organic matter content allows the production of seedlings with a well developed fibrous root system. In common with most woodland species the seeds of Ash tend to germinate relatively early in the spring and as frost and wind protection is naturally provided by the woodland canopy, it is important to provide such protection for an open seedbed. Although it is unusual for seedlings to be killed by frost their ultimate quality will be considerably reduced.

The Ashes do not appear to suffer from any unusual or specific pests and diseases in the seedbed.

ASSOCIATED READING

Barton, L.V. (1946) 'Viability of seeds of *Fraxinus* after storage', Contrib. Boyce Thompson Inst. *13*(9):427.
Steinbauer, G.P. (1937) 'Dormancy and germination of *Fraxinus* seeds', Plant Physiol. *12*.85.

Species	Dormancy Condition	Seedcount 000s/kg.
F. americana	E	
F. angustifolia	E	
F. excelsior	I + S + E	4 - 5
F. mariesii	E	
F. nigra	I + E	
F. ornus	E	50.0
F. oxycarpa	E	
F. pensylvanica	E	
F. pensylvanica lanceolata	E	
F. quadrangulata	I + E	
F. sieboldiana	E	

E = Embryo dormancy requiring chilling.
S = Hard seedcoat.
I = Immature embryo.
Dormancy conditions in various species of Ash

GINGKO

The Maidenhair Tree *(G. biloba)* is the only surviving member of this fossil species and on this account alone it would merit real attention. However it is also a highly ornamental and adaptable tree and is widely planted on these merits.

As a species it is dioecious and the production of seed therefore depends on the adjacent occurrence of both male and female trees. In the British Isles the tree is fairly widely planted and it has thrived in all but exposed locations. There are however relatively few reasonably old trees which are mature enough to fruit and as the majority of these are male trees, fruit is not commonly found. Fruit is produced on female trees in this country where old enough specimens are encountered.

The fruits of the species are yellow plum like structures which contain the single seeds, two or three fruits being borne at the end of the branchlets. These fruits emit an offensive odour when ripe and crushed, and it is for this reason that female trees are not commonly planted. Seeds are available from the normal commercial seed houses each year and these are collected in southern Europe quite readily.

The seeds should be bought annually as storage of the seeds is not easy. Successful short term storage (up to one year or so) is only achieved by mixing with damp peat and sealing in a polythene bag and keeping at cool (c. 3°C) temperatures. Dry storage is of no value as viability declines rapidly under these conditions.

Fresh seed should be sown each year as soon as it is received so that viability can be maintained. As embryo development is not completed until such time as the fruit is shed it would be unwise to pick fruit until it had reached this stage as extraction and the subsequent drying may well materially affect viability and embryo maturity.

The seeds do not possess any dormancy, but in common with many coniferous type subjects they benefit markedly from a period of chilling prior to germination. Seeds will germinate satisfactorily however without any such treatment, although the rate of emergence is significantly slower.

The seeds are relatively large (1.5 to 2 cm in diameter) and can be broadcast or station sown at a population of about 300 per square metre. Because of their size it is necessary to ensure that the seeds are firmly rolled in so that there is adequate contact for moisture uptake and the prevention of drying which is an important factor in successful production.

The seedlings are inevitably susceptible to frost damage and adequate protection must be provided.

The seedlings do not normally experience any particular pest and disease problems in the seedbed.

In most seasons growth is good and seedlings in the height range 20 to 30 cm are produced by leaf fall.

Species	Seedcount ,000s/kg
G. biloba	0.6

GLEDITSIA

This small genus of leguminous trees are more widely grown in suitable areas 113 of North America than the British Isles, largely on account of their suspect hardiness as young specimens. Of the so-called 'Honey Locusts' only *G. triacanthos* is at all commonly produced although occasionally *G. caspica* is offered. At the present time *G. triacanthos* 'Sunburst' is enjoying a period of popularity although its survival is probably enhanced by a succession of mild winters.

Seedling production is thus limited to *G. triacanthos* which is grown both as a rootstock and in its own right. *G. triacanthos inermis* which reproduces true to type from seed and *G. caspica* which is occasionally offered.

Seed of these are very rarely set in the British Isles, occasionally in very warm summers flower buds are set but rarely are the long succulent pods produced.

Seed, however, is readily obtainable from the commercial continental seedhouses and is normally available annually. The seed is typically leguminous and develops a hard and impermeable seedcoat so that storage from year to year can be easily achieved by dry storage at room temperature.

The only practical problem associated with the germination of seeds of this genus is concerned with the degree of hard seededness which has developed in the sample. Unless fresh seed is available it is usual to encounter a fair degree of hard seed coat development and to a level at which sulphuric acid digestion becomes a necessity.

The various sources of literature concerned with seedcoat digestion of these species offer widely divergent recommendations on the times required to reduce seedcoats. In effect these sources emphasise the variability which occurs both in degree of seedcoat development and the diversity of techniques involved and reiterates the importance of standardisation of operating technique and the individual assessement of each sample for treatment, so that each sample can be sown with an expectation of an adequate and effective germination.

Once the seedcoat has been reduced to a sufficient level, imbibition occurs rapidly and the seeds will often swell to some four times their dry volume. The seeds should be sown at this stage and any drying should be prevented. As the emerging seedlings are not frost hardy and as relatively warm temperatures are required for germination there is no necesssity to sow these species until late in the spring *viz.* early May.

The seeds are sown broadcast onto a conventional, prepared seedbed to achieve a population of about 350 plants per square metre.

The seedlings are remarkably free from pests and diseases in the seedbed and under normal circumstances do not receive any checks to growth.

Species	Seedcount ,000s/kg
G. caspica	8.0
G. triacanthos	7.0

GYMNOCLADUS DIOICUS

The 'Kentucky Coffee Tree' is the only representative of this genus to be found in cultivation in the British Isles, which has proved both sufficiently hardy and of real ornamental value. It is perfectly hardy in the southern half of the country but the summers are not sufficiently warm or bright enough for it to flower other than in exceptional circumstances.

Because of this it is not possible to obtain seed locally and recourse must be made to the commercial seedhouses. Seed is available from Southern European sources and is normally offered in most years.

Individually the seeds are large and typically leguminous in that they develop a hard seedcoat. Because of this habit they are readily stored dry in cool conditions and will retain viability and an acceptable degree of germination vigour for several years.

The only problem in germination of this subject is associated with the hard seedcoat condition. The degree of its development dictating seed treatment. Fresh seed can be germinated fairly readily if sown immediately after extraction as the seedcoat has not hardened to any significant extent and the seedlings will emerge in the spring. However, as seed is bought in dry from commercial seedhouses, the seedcoat will have hardened sufficiently to prevent germination in the first year and treatment to overcome this effect is necessary. Storage will also increase the degree of hardness.

Three alternative treatments are available depending on degree of hardness and the quantity to be dealt with. Small quantities can be dealt with by chipping individual seeds. Larger quantities can be hot water soaked for 24 hours and if the seed is fairly fresh most seeds will imbibe and the restrictive effect is overcome; seeds too hard for this treatment can be discarded. Seed which has been dry stored for more than one year will probably not submit to this treatment and will require digestion with sulphuric acid before the seeds will imbibe and germinate.

Experience suggests that seeds from Southern European sources, at least, do not require any exposure to cold temperature to encourage germination.

The seeds are individually large and can easily be space sown, the field factor will be high, as few seeds will fail to germinate if only the imbibed seed is sown. For this reason it would be wise not to sow until April in order to avoid exposure of the emerging seedlings to prolonged periods of frost.

Little data is available on plant densities and likely grades of one year old seedlings. However, a population of 400 per square metre on limited experience produces seedlings in the height range 20 to 30 cm.

Species	Seedcount ,000s/kg
G. dioicus	0.8-1.0

HAMAMELIS

The various 'Witch Hazels' are not normally produced from seed in the nursery trade but are more commonly propagated by vegetative methods. However, the commonest form of propagation employed is grafting and for this rootstocks are needed. As these are not satisfactorily produced vegetatively, seedling rootstocks are used.

The traditional rootstock for grafting Hamamelis has been *H. virginiana* largely because its foliage is reasonably distinct and contrasts with the scion varieties normally encountered (i.e. the asiatic species and hybrids), so that rootstock suckers can readily be identified. For various reasons seeds of this Witch Hazel are currently difficult to obtain from commercial sources and consequently are relatively expensive. This scarcity would appear to be chiefly due to the lack of collection rather than its availability. Commercial sources are not of course the only ones but local collection is often hampered by the lack of parent plants, as *H. virginiana* has rarely been planted as a specimen in its own right in British gardens. However, *H. mollis* has been widely planted and considerable quantities of seed are produced in most years on mature specimens and provided a suitable grafting technique is adopted could be used for rootstock purposes. Similarly *H. vernalis* is reasonably widely planted, sets fruit readily and could also be used as a rootstock if seedlings were not required for planting as specimens in their own right.

The fruit of Hamamelis at maturity is a reddish brown *(H. virginiana)* or fawn tomentose *(H. mollis)* capsule normally containing two shiny black seeds both of which are usually viable. The climate of the British Isles appears to permit the development of satisfactory crops in most warm years.

Witch Hazel seed does provide practical problems for the seedling propagator when obtained from commercial sources. Under natural circumstances the seeds are dispersed and germination occurs in the second spring after dispersal, however, the extended drying, cleaning and dry storage to which commercial samples are subjected enhances the seedcoat condition so that germination of much of the sample is retarded and occurs over several seasons. This pattern is fairly typical of those subjects exhibiting a hard or impermeable seedcoat condition coupled with embryo dormancy, which receive further artificial drying in storage.

This problem can be overcome by artificial means and two methods have been tried with varying degrees of success. The first involves a fairly lengthy period of warm stratification, for at least 12 weeks at a minimum of 60°F preferably with the diurnal fluctuations experienced under warm glasshouse conditions and followed by a period of chilling of at least 8 weeks duration. The second depends on the successful reduction of the seedcoat by acid digestion and a subsequent chilling treatment, however this technique has not proved very successful using a sulphuric acid digestion, but this is not uncommon with subjects in which the seedcoat is 'tough' as opposed to 'hard'. Nitric acid has proved more successful with other subjects (viz. *Tilia)* and may be more successful with these species as sulphuric acid only produces an etching action. These treatments are time consuming and costly and if not regularly monitored can result in losses during stratification due to water logging and/or rotting.

The most successful method of pretreatment is in avoiding the development of the seedcoat condition by collecting the fruits while they are still 'green'. This does however involve a somewhat tedious manual extraction of the seed but provided the seed is prevented from drying and sown without delay, germination the following spring is high (80-90%). As with other subjects in which hard seedcoat conditions are avoided by collection prior to ripening, the assessment of that period at which embryo maturity and completed storage of food is reached is the critical factor. It is difficult to be conclusive from the limited evidence available but in England this stage is usually reached certainly by the second half of August and seeds collected and sown then have yielded good results. It may be quite possible however to collect considerably earlier, as the early flowering habit may have produced early seed production although the development of the fruit component is immature *(cf. Daphne)*: this however would provide problems of extraction unless fruits were sown whole.

If seeds are sown early then it is important to ensure that the seedbed is kept moist to prevent any possibility of the fruit drying out and the hard seedcoat developing.

The seeds are sown broadcast onto a prepared seedbed, preferably with a high leaf mould content and reasonably acidic in reaction. The seed should be firmed in to ensure water uptake and imbibition, and then covered with grit.

A population of 200 to 250 per square metre will produce seedlings of adequate size.

The only consistent pest encountered is the aphid although various bugs and thrips can cause trouble in some years.

Species	Seedcount in ,000s/kg
H. virginiana	$20.0 \pm 10\%$

HIBISCUS

The genus *Hibiscus* is a large and diverse group of mostly tropical or subtropical trees and shrubs; a few species of which are reputedly hardy, but only *H. syriacus* is usually seen in cultivation in the British gardens. This species is shrubby in habit and is extremely variable in its flower colouration so that normal propagation practice is to produce selected cultivars vegetatively. Vegetative propagation is carried out by layering — which is not a commercially viable practice; by stem cuttings — which are slow to strike and establish; or by grafting. This last technique requires a rootstock and it is for this purpose that seedlings are produced. Normally an unsophisticated, wedge graft on a one year old seedling will suffice and seedling production is therefore geared to the development of material suitable for this purpose. The ideal product is a one year old seedling with a hypocotyl diameter of the order 4 to 6 mm.

Seed can be purchased from conventional commercial sources and is readily available, however, it is also very easily collected in the local situation. Once plants of selected cultivars have been established they will normally flower profusely and set seed. However, fruit production may be hampered by an unfavourable autumn, as such a late flowering subject would obviously be prone. It is also a late flushing subject and in areas where growth is restricted it may be necessary to establish stock plants under glass or polythene in order to produce adequate stem growth for use as scions. These plants will also flower on the older wood and develop fruits quite readily so that seed can be collected late in the season without difficulty. The 117 pods can be left late on the plants until they are well dried out and at this stage will begin to open and liberate the seeds: if collected at this stage and broken up the seeds can easily be separated by coarse sieving or picking over and then winnowing.

The seeds normally exhibit a high level of viability (c. 90%) and do not possess any dormancy controls which effectively delay germination under practical conditions. The seeds germinate readily as soon as temperatures rise to a sufficient level in the spring. Germination tests to establish emergence are easily conducted under closed case conditions. It is important to ensure that the seeds are well firmed into the compost so that the hardest seedcoat is readily soaked and imbibition occurs without delay.

The seeds are broadcast onto a conventional seedbed to produce a population of 400 + /sq. m., and provided adequate protection is available will grow steadily to reach the required size by the end of the season.

In the seedbed the seedlings are inevitably subject to frost damage. As far as pests are concerned the main problem is posed by aphids which can develop epidemic populations in a very short time on these subjects. Otherwise only 'Damping off' conditions at emergence are likely to be problematical.

Species	Seedcount ,000s/kg
H. syriacus	53.0

ILEX

The Hollies are a variable group of evergreen trees and shrubs of wide geographical distribution throughout the north temperate regions of the world. They have produced problems for the seedling propagator for generations and are one of the most difficult genera to raise from seed with any speed, reliability, consistency or success. However, since most of the hollies are grown as forms selected for shape, foliage colour or berry production, they are customarily propagated vegetatively in order to perpetuate these characteristics. Seedlings are normally only required for hedging purposes and occasionally, as demand arises, as rootstocks. It is unusual to encounter specimen seedlings as the Holly species are normally dioecious and as the sex of the tree cannot be determined until the mature phase is reached after eight to ten years, its fruiting potential will be unknown.

The fruit of the Holly is the well recognised berry which in the case of *I. aquifolium* will contain from one to four seeds, depending on pollination, fertilisation and subsequent climatic conditions. It matures in the late autumn to early winter and dispersal is by birds, in most seasons the fruit is not taken until into the New Year and the crop can quite successfully be picked by hand from the tree; any periodicity of production which appears to occur seems to be a function of the vagaries of the climate rather than any inherent rhythm. The limiting problem of seedling production in Holly is associated with the particularly complex dormancy controls which will often delay germination and emergence of the greater part of a seed sample until the third or fourth spring after dispersal. Dormancy is caused by:—

(i) a particularly tough and intractable seedcoat,
(ii) an immature embryo of the undifferentiated type and
(iii) the development of a chilling requirement in the matured embryo.

So that, in effect, before germination can occur the seed must first have its seed coat reduced to allow imbibition and aeration, at which stage if it is subjected to warm conditions for a sufficient period, maturation of the embryo will occur: finally the embryo must be exposed to a period of chilling; after all these requirements have been fulfilled exposure to normal environmental conditions suitable for germination will promote the emergence of the seedling.

Many possible courses of action are available to the propagator in order to promote germination as quickly and as evenly as possible. Sulphuric acid digestion can be used but care is necessary if damage to the internal parts of the seed is to be avoided, subsequent to such digestion the seed must be subjected to warm stratification in order to mature the embryo, thus it may be more acceptable to simply expose the stratified seed to warm temperatures for an extended period in order to achieve both effects. Adequate reduction of the seedcoat together with embryo maturation can be achieved if the extracted seed is stratified soon after collection and kept in warm glasshouse conditions, (diurnal range 60° - 90°F) until the following autumn (for air/water/medium rations see page 61). The seed could then be sown so that chilling is achieved in the seedbed; however it would appear that holly seeds require exposure to a fairly severe chill and this may be more satisfactorily acquired by cold storage until a spring sowing as the current cycle of mild winters do not provide a sufficient chill during one winter to break dormancy control.

At sowing the seeds are broadcast to achieve a population of 350-400 seedlings per square metre. Sowing should not be delayed until too far on in the spring as high soil temperatures may induce a secondary dormancy in freshly sown chilled seed.

Hollies do not appear to suffer from any particular problems in the seedbed.

Species	Seedcount ,000s/kg
I. aquifolium	25.0

ASSOCIATED READING

Giersbach, J. and W. Crocker (1929) 'Germination of Ilex seeds', Amer. J. Bot. *16*:854.
Orton, E.R., Jr., Davis, S.H., Jr. and L. M. Vasvary (1966) 'Growing American Holly in New Jersey', N.J. Agr. Ext. Bull. *388*.
Ives, S.A. (1923) 'Maturation and germination of seeds of *Ilex opaca*', Bot. Gaz. *76*:60.

JUGLANS

The Walnuts are usually represented in cultivation in the British Isles by *J. regia* (the Persian or English Walnut) and *J. nigra* (the Black Walnut) which   119 both develop into large trees of considerable stature once they become established. Fruiting specimens of both species can be found although the former is much more widely planted. Fruiting varieties of the English Walnut are offered in the nursery trade and these are normally produced by grafting onto a rootstock.

These plants are usually propagated from seed for specimens in their own right and *J. regia* is also grown as a seedling for rootstock purposes.

The fruit of the Walnut is a fleshy husk surrounding the familiar nut. The fruit is shed whole and at this stage the pith is disintegrating and rotting leaving the nut free. The seed is collected by picking up from the ground and rubbing away the husks. It is advisable to wear gloves for this job as the flesh contains a persistent dark stain. The seeds are then floated to wash away any further detritus and to test for soundness.

Walnut seeds do not withstand drying very satisfactorily and viability deteriorates rapidly in dry storage. Moist storage by mixing damp peat with the seed, sealing in a polythene bag and keeping at 1 to 3°C extends useful life of the seed to about 12 months. Seeds of *J. regia* are more susceptible to drying than *J. nigra*.

Seeds of the Walnuts will germinate satisfactorily if spring sown and do not appear to possess any embryo dormancy requiring chilling. However, germination is more rapid, uniform and successful if the seeds are exposed to a chilling period prior to exposure to those conditions which would encourage germination.

In practice most satisfactory germination results from autumn sowing, although storage at low temperature over the winter as described, followed by spring sowing will achieve the same effect. Stratification of the nuts can be employed, but as germination may occur whenever conditions are warm enough the radical may well emerge while still in the bin, and this makes sowing more difficult although not impossible. It is important therefore that stratified seed should be regularly monitored.

The chief problem with autumn sowing is the prevention of loss to rodents and birds over the winter but this can be reduced to minimal levels by rolling out windbreak netting over the beds, or by dressing or tainting the nuts.

The seedlings are particularly susceptible to frost and it is important to provide some form of cover from the time the seedlings begin to emerge.

The seeds are large and can reasonably easily be station sown. If the seedbed is prepared and left unfirmed the seeds can be placed and then rolled or pressed into the soil so that good contact for water uptake can be achieved. The bed is then covered with grit to maintain good aeration.

The seeds are large and the resulting seedlings, although not tall, have a fat hypocotyl and so populations are not high; a reasonable level being about 200 + per square metre.

Seed size from year to year is very variable both from commercial and home sources although seed from British trees tend to vary considerably being on the periphery of climate suitable for annual seed production.

Species	Seeds/kg
J. nigra	40 ± 20
J. regia	45 ± 15

ASSOCIATED READING

Barton, L.V. (1936) 'Seedling Production in *Carya ovata* (Mill.) K. Koch, *Juglans cinerea* L., and *Juglans nigra* L.' Contrib. Boyce Thompson Inst. *8*:1.
Stuke, W. (1960) 'Seed and seed handling techniques in the production of walnut seedlings', Proc. Plant Prop. Soc. *10*:274.

KOELREUTERIA

K. paniculata, the Goldenrain Tree, is a not uncommon tree in cultivation in the British Isles, although good, well established flowering specimens are relatively few and far between. Seed production is, under normal circumstances, unusual in this climate.

Seed is readily available annually from the usual commercial seed houses and is supplied as clean samples with virtually no impurities. The seed can be stored, if necessary, quite satisfactorily dry at normal room temperatures and viability is retained over several years.

The seed is generally of good quality with viability well over 90 per cent. The seed of this subject would appear to present difficulties to the propagator as the literature suggests that it possesses both a hard seedcoat and an embryo dormancy; but the author has sown seed under warm glasshouse conditions with no apparent detriment to germination. However, some samples of seed do develop hard seedcoats which will become increasingly intractable especially if the seed has been dried.

The hard seededness can be dealt with according to its severity, if fresh seed from the current season's crop is available a simple 24 hour soak prior to sowing will cause imbibition, if this is not effective a period of warm water treatment will normally overcome the problem. The seeds should be covered with nearly boiling water which is left to cool in a warm place so that the water is kept warm. When the sample of seed has developed a hard seedcoat which will not respond to these treatments, it will be necessary to resort to sulphuric acid digestion, however, it will normaliy only require a relatively short period of action before the coat is reduced.

Although it has been indicated that germination has been achieved in warm glasshouse conditions it may be that, in common with several other subjects, germination will occur at high temperatures despite the presence of embryo dormancy. It would therefore be prudent to sow this subject early in an outdoor seedbed so that the embryo chilled and perhaps improve both the level and rate of germination.

Species	Seedcount ,000s/kg
K. paniculata	7.0

LABURNUM

Two species of this easily grown genus of leguminous, small trees are encountered in cultivation; however their popularity is somewhat on the decline because of their poisonous nature, especially the seeds which tend to be eaten by children. The very floriferiousness of their growth nevertheless maintains demand at reasonable levels.

The 'Scotch Laburnum' *(L. alpinum)* and the 'Common Laburnum' *(L. anagyroides)* are both commonly grown from seed in their own right although the latter is also used as a rootstock for working the large flowered hybrids, *L. x watereri,* and *L. x vossii.* The seeds which are produced in abundance annually, develop in a typical leguminous pod containing about 7 seeds. These are shed in the autumn by pod explosion and it is necessary to collect the pods before dispersal so that the seeds can be extracted easily. If the pods are dried the seeds are fairly readily separated by flailing.

The seeds are small, dark in colour and typically leguminous in appearance, however although they possess a hard seedcoat it is not impermeable once the seed has been soaked and there is normally no delay to germination.

The seed does not exhibit any particular dormancy conditions and can be spring sown with a good germination. The seed is generally sound and no great losses should be expected.

Sowing broadcast onto a prepared seedbed so that a population of about 350 plants per square metre produces trees of acceptable size.

The seedlings are hardy and grow vigorously, suffering from virtually no pest and disease problems in the seedbed.

Species	Seedcount ,000s/kg
L. anagyroides	40

LIQUIDAMBAR

Only one species of this Hamamelid is commonly seen in cultivation in the British Isles — the 'Sweet Gum' *(L. styraciflua).* This tree is native of the eastern parts of North America with a considerable north/south geographical distribution. When selecting an imported source of seed for growing in Britain it is prudent to obtain seeds of the hardier northern strains.

Seed is occasionally produced on trees in the United Kingdom but the quantity available appears to be governed by the number of sufficiently mature trees and the warmth of the summer. The increasing appearance of fruits on specimens planted locally over the last ten years or so, can be attributed to the fact that many trees appear to have been planted during the first two or three decades of the century and are now well into maturity. The warm summers of 1975 and 1976 have also induced good crops. *Liquidambar* would appear, however, to crop reasonably consistently provided that climatic conditions at flowering and fruit set are not uncongenial.

122 The fruits mature in late October and November and should be collected

as they turn yellow so that the seeds can be collected before dispersal. The fruits are dried in a warm place and extracted by shaking, experience of reasonably good crops suggests about five or six seeds will be obtained per fruit. The seeds are small, light and winged.

The seeds require a period of chilling to overcome embryo dormancy and this is almost satisfactorily achieved by sowing after collection, however seed may necessarily have to be imported and this should be sown or stratified to obtain three months chilling.

Viability of the seeds is not always good and can be as low as 50%.

At sowing these small, light, winged seeds should be pressed or rolled into the soil thoroughly, so that contact for moisture uptake is achieved.

Seedling management is unexceptional and a population of about 300 per square metre is adequate.

Species	Seedcount ,000s/kg
L. styraciflua	$200 \pm 25\%$

ASSOCIATED READING

Wilcox, J.R. (1968) 'Sweetgum seed stratification requirements related to winter climate at seed source' Forest Sci. *14*:16.

LIRIODENDRON

The 'Tulip Tree' *(L. tulipifera)* is the only species of this genus which is at all commonly encountered in cultivation in the British Isles. It is a native of the North American continent where it is known as the 'Yellow Poplar' and has been extensively planted. It is much more widely grown in these islands than is commonly supposed and proves to be considerably hardier once established than is normally anticipated. Once established it grows with reasonable vigour and has even succeeded as an avenue planting in such a rigorous environment at Chatsworth in Derbyshire. The only other species, *L. chinense,* has not succeeded here except in the milder conditions of the south west, it is a native of central China and suffers from the effects of late spring frost as it commonly flushes vigorously into growth once temperatures rise in the spring.

The yellow magnolia like flowers of the Tulip tree are produced in June and the fruit matures in the autumn. The fruit is cone like and breaks up to shed the seeds in the early winter period. Fruiting in the British climate is very spasmodic and usually only occurs in very hot summers. Seed production when it occurs, is extraordinarily prolific but a very small proportion is sound, often as low as one per cent. The seed is long and winged, and is not unlike an Ash key in appearance. The seeds are in fact winged carpels, orginally with two seeds of which one aborts. The food store is largely endospermic and is very oily.

Commercial seed has very low viability generally, because of the normally inherent proportion of unsound, void seed and because short term storage prior to despatch is usually warm and dry and the oily nature of the food reserve deteriorates rapidly. The seeds exhibit a conventional cold temperature embryo dormancy which requires a period of chilling before germination will occur. Fresh seed, therefore, sown in the autumn will germinate the following spring. However seed from commercial sources which has been dried and stored often shows a delayed dormancy due, it would appear, to the marginal development of an impermeable seedcoat so that a period of warm temperature stratification is needed to overcome this.

There is virtually no need to store *Liriodendron* seed as supplies are available from most commercial sources on a regular annual basis.

The seed is broadcast onto the seedbed to achieve a population of 250 to 300 seedlings per square metre. This implies a fairly thick layer of seed which must be rolled to ensure adequate contact with the soil for imbibition of water.

Seed size is variable but is usually about 30,000 seeds per kilogram.

ASSOCIATED READING

Boyce, S., C. and M. Kaieser, (1961) 'Why yellow — poplar seeds have low viability' Central Sta. For. Exp. Sta. U.S.D.A. Tech. Paper *186*.
Giersbach, J. (1929) 'The effect of stratification on seeds of *Liriodendron tulipifera*' Amer. Jour. Bot. *16*:835.
Guard, A.T. and R.E. Wean (1941) 'Seed production in Tulip Poplar', J. For. *39*:1032.
Hinson, E. (1935) 'The collection of Yellow Poplar seed', J. For. *33*:1007.
Wean, R.E. and A.T. Guard (1940) 'The Viability and collection of seed of *Liriodendron tulipifera* L.', J. For. *38*:815.

MAGNOLIA

The propagation of Magnolias from seed is limited to the production of rootstocks for grafting and for the development of new varieties and hybrids in a breeding programme. Most species can be propagated from seed but the length of time between germination and flowering is, in most cases, so extended that it is not a feasible commercial proposition, especially as the quality of flower production is not invariably satisfactory. Thus the number of species of Magnolia which are grown commercially from seed is normally limited to *M. acuminata, M. kobus,* occasionally *M. virginiana* and the evergreen *M. grandiflora*.

Mature seed bearing trees of these species can be found with reasonable frequency in the British Isles although they are usually only encountered in the larger private gardens and specialist parks, inevitably their occurrence is more frequent in the favoured climatic conditions of the South West. However mature specimens are nevertheless found in many sheltered gardens in other parts of the country.

The chief problem in obtaining seed from such sources is that by no means do all mature specimens set viable seeds and that as most mature magnolias are likely to be single and isolated specimens of their species it is probable that fertile seed will only be set if the plant self pollinates, *M. acuminata* is especially intriguing in this respect having several clones of differing pollination requirements.